BUSINESS INFORMATION SYSTEM ARCHITECTURE

PAUL GREFEN

Front cover illustration:
Blue Glass Wall
Science Museum, London, UK
Architecture with Information Elements
(Photo by author)

Published by Grefen Digital Business Architecture
Eindhoven, The Netherlands

PREFACE

Architecture of business information systems – or just of information systems – is an important field in information systems research, but even more so in business practice. Information (as a 'distilled' form of data) is getting increasingly important to many organizations – profit and non-profit alike. But the 'art' of properly shaping the systems that manage and process this information remains an often badly represented capability. This book is meant to contribute to developing this capability.

Positioning of this book

Business information system architecture is positioned between the better understood fields of enterprise architecture and software architecture. As explained in Chapter 2 of this book, enterprise architecture is generally of a more abstract nature – and quite often results in large sets of very detailed models of various views on information management in an organization. Organizing information systems in their mutual relations is not the focal point here. Software architecture is much more technical, focusing on the work of software engineers. This field typically focuses on lower aggregation levels, i.e., at the 'inside' of business information systems. The field of this book balances between the two, trying to be not overly technical but reasoning in terms of structures of systems, and also trying to focus on a level of complexity (and hence aggregation) where insight does not get lost too quickly.

Given this balance, one can consider the contents of this book to be based on a 'middle-out' approach, where enterprise architecture is often top-down and software architecture bottom-up (to paint things admittedly a bit black-and-white). This middle-out approach is getting increasingly important in a world where we see two major developments. On the one hand, we see that the 'make-or-buy' question in realizing information systems is more and more answered with the 'buy' decision: developing situation-specific systems becomes less and less feasible for a variety of reasons. On the other hand, we see that information processing in modern organizations has become that complex, that no single bought system can realize all required functionality. Consequently, compounds of standard systems have to be carefully designed by choosing the right elements and connections. This is right in the heart of this book.

This book is to a large extent language-agnostic. Yes, it is written in the English language – but this is not the point here. It is agnostic with respect to architecture specification languages (and frameworks), like ArchiMate. We do explain some languages and frameworks in this book, though (in Chapter 5 to be precise). To remain language-agnostic, we mostly use pragmatic specification techniques in this book, where clarity prevails over formal syntactical considerations.

Purpose of this book

This book provides a general introduction into the field of architecture of business information systems (or corporate information systems) at the M.Sc. level. This field contains many topics and many aspects, ranging from business-oriented elements to technology-oriented elements and from architectures of small component systems to architectures of multi-national corporate information systems. The main purpose of this book is to provide a structured overview of these topics and aspects and explain the interrelationships between them. This means that not all individual elements can be elaborated to a great depth. For deep elaborations of elements, readers are referred to other work – the references in the text of this book and the bibliography at the end of this book provide a first point of entry for this purpose.

Target audience of this book

The main target audience of the book is formed by M.Sc. students in a business engineering curriculum with some background in the field of information systems and M.Sc. students in a computer science curriculum with interest in technology application in business contexts. The book is interesting as well for Ph.D. students and other researchers who need to design complex business information systems in their projects.

As the topic of business information system analysis and design is very relevant for any mid- or large-size organization, the book also targets business professionals in practice, such as business analysts, senior software engineers, junior information system architects and digital business transformation consultants.

History of this book

As explained in the beginning of this preface, business information system architecture is an important field, but also caught in between other fields. When starting teaching the field (long ago), there was no appropriate book available. So the choice was simple: develop your own material – which was done. And even now, after quite some years, there is to the best of my knowledge still no other book that covers the domain in the middle-out way described before. Hence, I have kept developing own material. The most recent incarnation of this material is now before you.

Earlier versions of this book have been developed by the author as course material for the Business Information System Architecture (BISA) course (1BM41/1BM47) taught at the School of Industrial Engineering of Eindhoven University of Technology (TU/e) in the Netherlands at the MSc and PhD levels.

Older roots of this course go even back to the course on Architecture of Complex Information Systems (ACIS) that the author co-taught at the University of Twente quite some years ago by now – so there is quite some experience behind the material in this book. Obviously, the contents have been adapted through the times to follow developments in both the science and the application domains.

Earlier versions of this book have been published internally at TU/e, with some copies going 'outside' on an individual basis. As there have been multiple requests to make the material available on a broader scale, it is now offered through commercial channels. The contents of the current version of the book have been heavily updated and extended to provide a complete and contemporary overview of the field. I do hope that many will enjoy this book in years to come.

Paul Grefen
Eindhoven, 2025

ACKNOWLEDGMENTS

Several professionals have contributed to the development of the contents of this book. Rik Eshuis of Eindhoven University of Technology, Richard Lendvai of Atos Origin (at that moment), Danny Greefhorst of ArchiXL, and Paul Brandt of TNO are thanked for their feedback on various elements of previous versions of the TU/e-internal predecessor of this book.

My discussions with (former) TU/e students about architecture have also greatly helped in pinpointing things right. Special mention goes to Anna Lyubchenko and Vassil Stoitsev. Astrid van den Bos is thanked for identifying a list of errors in a previous, internally published version of the book.

Henk Blanken of the University of Twente back then is thanked for introducing me to teaching in the field of information system architecture – which was quite in its infancy in those days.

Ton Soetekouw of Xibix (and formerly ING Bank) is thanked for inspiring me (and pushing me a bit) to finally publish my material as a publicly available book – in which he has obviously succeeded now.

I have had numerous discussions with colleagues – both in the academic world and in the industrial world – that have helped shape the contents of this book. These colleagues are too many to all be mentioned here, but I thank them nevertheless for their knowledge and opinions.

TABLE OF CONTENTS

1   INTRODUCTION 1

1.1   The focus of this book 1
1.2   The structure of this book 2

2   THE CONCEPT OF ARCHITECTURE 5

2.1   Architecture as an approach for structure 5
   2.1.1   The characteristics of modern information systems 6
   2.1.2   The need for structure 7
   2.1.3   The legacy problem 8
   2.1.4   The greenfield problem 9
   2.1.5   Extending and restraining information systems 9
2.2   The two faces of architecture 10
2.3   Architecture as a structural blueprint 12
   2.3.1   Architecture of a software system 13
   2.3.2   Architecture of a (corporate) information system 13
2.4   Architecture more precisely 14
   2.4.1   Architecture as a set of models 14
   2.4.2   Architecture as a system 15
2.5   Other types of architectures 16
   2.5.1   Architecture in building 16
   2.5.2   Architecture in computer science 19
   2.5.3   Enterprise architecture 21
2.6   The IS architect 22
2.7   Architecture as a business agility instrument 24

3   UNDERSTANDING ARCHITECTURES IN
    DIMENSIONS 27

3.1   A set of architecture dimensions 27
3.2   Aspect dimension 28
   3.2.1   The notion of aspect 29
   3.2.2   The Truijens 5 aspects framework 29
   3.2.3   A modern variation on the Truijens framework 31
   3.2.4   Specifying aspect architectures 32
   3.2.5   Example application case of the UT5 framework 34
   3.2.6   The Kruchten 4+1 aspect framework 40
   3.2.7   UT5 versus K4+1 42

3.2.8   The formal view revisited..43
3.3   Aggregation dimension 44
3.3.1   Principles...44
3.3.2   Examples..46
3.3.3   The formal view revisited.....................................52
3.4   Abstraction dimension..53
3.4.1   Principles...53
3.4.2   Examples..54
3.4.3   Aggregation versus abstraction 58
3.5   Realization dimension 59
3.6   Combining dimensions into a design space......................60
3.6.1   A four-dimensional design space 61
3.6.2   A three-dimensional design cube 62
3.6.3   An alternative three-dimensional cube 66
3.6.4   Traversing the design space in a structured way......69

4   UNDERSTANDING ARCHITECTURES IN STRUCTURES 71

4.1   Architecture styles...72
4.1.1   The concept of architecture style 73
4.1.2   A simple software aspect style catalogue..............73
4.1.3   Layered style 74
4.1.4   Columned style...77
4.1.5   Component-oriented style 80
4.1.6   Combining styles...82
4.1.7   Styles in an application example............................83
4.1.8   Styles for other architecture aspects....................86
4.1.9   The formal view revisited......................................87
4.2   Architecture patterns 87
4.2.1   The concept of architecture pattern......................88
4.2.2   Patterns for the software aspect............................89
4.2.3   A simple pattern catalog for the software aspects ...90
4.2.4   A hierarchical pattern catalog for the software aspect............91
4.2.5   Relating pattern catalogs 94
4.2.6   Patterns in an application example 95
4.2.7   Patterns for other aspects 97
4.3   Reference architectures 98
4.3.1   The concept of reference architecture 100
4.3.2   Reference architectures for individual systems.......102
4.3.3   Reference architectures for enterprise integration ..105
4.3.4   Reference architectures for inter-organizational integration.. 107
4.3.5   Reference architectures for other architecture aspects 110
4.3.6   Reference architectures versus standard architectures 111

5   ARCHITECTING WITH RECIPES.................................115

5.1   Architecture design frameworks 116

   5.1.1   Zachman framework...117
   5.1.2   MDA framework 119

5.2   Architecture specification techniques 120

   5.2.1   UML 121
   5.2.2   ArchiMate...121

5.3   Architecture design approaches 123

   5.3.1   Top-down versus bottom-up design.........................123
   5.3.2   Dealing with aspects 124
   5.3.3   Agile system development.......................................125

5.4   Architecture design methods.......................................126

   5.4.1   TOGAF ADM 126
   5.4.2   COMET 127

5.5   Architecture principles..127

   5.5.1   Greefhorst and Proper catalog 128

6   DISTINGUISHING BETWEEN APPLICATIONS AND INFRASTRUCTURES 131

6.1   Application and infrastructure layers............................132

   6.1.1   Layering applications and infrastructure................132
   6.1.2   Relation to multi-tier architectures 133

6.2   Application layer elements...135

   6.2.1   Modularization of the application layer.................135
   6.2.2   Porter's value chain model 136
   6.2.3   An application layer structure................................137

6.3   Infrastructure layer elements.......................................139

   6.3.1   Modularization of the infrastructure layer.............140
   6.3.2   Support system classification 140
   6.3.3   An infrastructure layer structure...........................140

6.4   Application and infrastructure architecting processes 141

   6.4.1   Application and infrastructure lifecycles 141
   6.4.2   Economics of applications and infrastructures........142
   6.4.3   Application and infrastructure architects..............142

7   ARCHITECTURES OF CONCRETE SYSTEMS 145

7.1   Data warehousing architecture.....................................146

   7.1.1   Reference architecture..146
   7.1.2   Concrete architecture...149

7.2   Business process management architecture 151

7.2.1   *WfMC reference architecture*.................................... *151*
7.2.2   *Mercurius reference architecture* *152*
7.2.3   *Concrete architecture* *153*
7.3   Application system architecture 155
7.3.1   *Architecture structure* *155*
7.3.2   *Interoperability patterns in the application architecture*......... *156*
7.3.3   *Application architectures in enterprise architecting* *159*

8   TECHNOLOGIES FOR ARCHITECTURE EMBODIMENT 163

8.1   Application system technologies 164
8.1.1   *Make-oriented technologies* *164*
8.1.2   *Buy-oriented technologies* *165*
8.2   Infrastructure system technologies 165
8.2.1   *Database management technology* *166*
8.2.2   *Business process management technology*................ *169*
8.3   The place of embodiment discussions 170

9   MIDDLEWARE TECHNOLOGIES 173

9.1   The need for middleware.. 173
9.1.1   *Connecting application systems*............................ *174*
9.1.2   *Connecting application and infrastructure systems*................ *176*
9.2   What is middleware? 177
9.3   Database-oriented middleware 179
9.4   Function-oriented middleware....................................... 180
9.5   Message-oriented middleware 181
9.6   Object-oriented middleware 182
9.6.1   *CORBA*.. *182*
9.6.2   *DCOM*... *186*
9.7   Service-oriented middleware... 187
9.7.1   *Web Service technology* *187*
9.7.2   *A simple Web Service application scenario* *189*
9.7.3   *SOA and ESB* *190*
9.8   Introducing middleware into an application landscape 190
9.8.1   *Greenfield versus legacy scenarios*........................ *191*
9.8.2   *Evolution towards middleware* *192*

10   ARCHITECTURE IN RETROSPECTIVE 195

10.1   The importance of IS architecture 195
10.2   Challenges of the IS Architect...................................... 196

11 REFERENCES..199

12 ABOUT THE AUTHOR.......................................207

13 INDEX...209

14 TABLE OF FIGURES...215

1 INTRODUCTION

In this short introductory chapter, we first discuss the content focus of this book and its information systems engineering point of view. After that, we explain the structure of this book in terms of its chapters and the contents of these.

1.1 The focus of this book

This book is about the architecture of business information systems, i.e., about the structure of computerized systems that underlie the operation of any complex modern organization (or business network of collaborating organizations [Gre16]). Typically, these systems are of substantial (and increasing) complexity, such that attention for their organization in specific structures is essential to develop, install and use them properly.

The book is focused heavily on the structuring perspective, i.e., how to analyze and design complex architectures in a well-organized fashion. The analysis and design cannot be performed without proper background in concepts, models, techniques and tools. The focus of this book is exactly on these elements, where we try to create as much as possible cohesion between them.

Where architecture in building is often concerned with beautifying and creating (visual) tension (see for example Figure 1), business information system architecture is concerned with simplifying and removing tension. In other words: building architecture is rooted in art, business information system architecture is rooted in engineering. Consequently, this book presents an *architecture engineering* point of view.

Figure 1: Guggenheim Museum, Bilbao, Spain, designed by Frank Gehry (photo by author)

1.2 The structure of this book

This book has been designed to have a clear chapter structure that moves from the basics of information system architecture to the more advanced topics. The structure of this book is as follows:

Chapter 2 introduces the concept of information system architecture and places it into various perspectives.

Chapter 3 presents a multi-dimensional framework that is used to understand the structure of complex architectures (as usually encountered in practice). As such, it offers a 'conceptual analyzing framework' for the information system architect.

Chapter 4 discusses structures for the design of architectures, thereby offering a 'conceptual building toolbox' for the information system architect.

Chapter 5 is devoted to design approaches for information system architectures, which offer 'practical construction guidelines' for the architect.

Chapter 6 pays attention to the important difference between infrastructure architecture and application architecture.

Chapter 7 discusses architectures of concrete information systems. In doing so, it employs concepts from the preceding chapters.

Chapter 8 discusses information technologies for architecture embodiment, i.e., software technologies for the realization of information systems described by architectures.

Chapter 9 focuses on middleware technologies, i.e., technologies that can be used to integrate information system components as defined by an architecture.

Chapter 10 contains the conclusions of this book, in which we place the concepts of business information system architecture and the role of the IS architect in retrospective.

The structure of the book is illustrated in Figure 2. Here we see that Chapters 2 through 5 form a cluster devoted to 'concepts', Chapters 6 and 7 form a cluster focusing on 'applications', and Chapters 8 and 9 are devoted to 'realization' of architectures (where 'realization' refers to the actual implementation of systems described by architectures, also referred to as 'embodiment' as noted above).

The field of information system architecture is a complex field with many points of view (as will see later in this book) and many interrelationships between concepts. Therefore, for students it is recommended to read this book in the order of the chapters as presented. When using the book as reference material, having a general overview of the information system architecture domain, this is obviously less important.

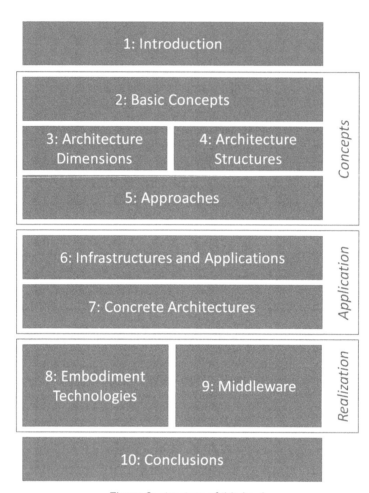

Figure 2: structure of this book

2 THE CONCEPT OF ARCHITECTURE

In this chapter, we discuss the nature of the architecture concept in the field of information systems. We explain that architecture is mainly related to structuring the design (both process and product) of complex information systems. We first investigate why there is actually a need for structure. Then, we discuss the two faces of architecture that are related to the process and product aspects of designing information systems. Next, we introduce architecture as a structural blueprint for complex information systems and define the concept of architecture. We then provide a more theoretical context by discussing architecture from the modeling and system theory perspectives. To put things into practical perspective, we next spend a few words on architecture of other artifacts – showing that there are many similarities to the information systems domain, but also a number of important differences. We end this chapter with a discussion of the role of the information system architect.

2.1 Architecture as an approach for structure

Architecture in general is about structure. Information system architecture is about structure of information systems. Before we dive into the specifics of this structure, it is first good to know why we actually need this structure. This section addresses this issue from three points of view. First, we take a general look at the characteristics of modern information systems to understand their inherent complexity. Secondly, we explain why this creates a need for structure – and the process of structuring. Then, we take a look at problems created in the past (so-called *legacy problems*), which require extra attention to structure towards the future. Next, we look at what appears the opposite situation: the *greenfield* situation where systems are designed for new organizations that start small but hope to grow large. Finally, we look at extending information systems to meet future requirements and the forces that play in the field of these extensions.

2.1.1 The characteristics of modern information systems

In the distant past (which for information systems means a few decades ago), information systems were usually of limited complexity and of limited connectivity. They typically supported the basic operation of a limited set of administrative business functions, like general ledger and payroll administration. They were typically connected to few other information systems in a very simple way (if at all), often using off-line connections (e.g., using magnetic tape as a transport medium). Such a rather disconnected system is sometimes referred to as a *silo* of functionality.

In the present time, individual information systems have become of far greater complexity as they support far more aspects of an extended set of business functions. To support end-to-end business processes, they are often connected to a myriad of other information systems, both within the same organization and across organizational boundaries. Individual information systems are arranged (often connected) into an 'information system landscape' – together they form a *complex information system*, also called *corporate information system[1]* (both abbreviated to CIS).

To give an idea of its size and complexity, a CIS for a large organization typically

- consist of hundreds of individual information systems for specific functions, each of which is of considerable complexity too;

- has a complex structure of interconnections (interfaces) between these individual systems;

- has a large (and growing) set of interfaces to external information systems, i.e., information systems managed by external organizations;

- runs on a broad range of IT platforms, part of which can be of a legacy nature (i.e., do not conform to modern standards and hence bring their own problems in terms of maintainability);

- has a huge (and quickly growing) set of functional requirements stating what the system should do (i.e., listing its functions in detail);

- has a large (and quickly growing too) set of nonfunctional requirements stating how the system should perform its tasks (e.g., in terms of performance, availability and security);

---

[1] Note that we could also use the term *enterprise information system*. We don't use this term here, as it may cause confusion with the term *enterprise resource planning system (ERP system)*. An ERP system can be part of a corporate information system (in many organizations, it is a very important part).

- is managed and maintained by a department that can range from a few hundred to a few thousand professionals, often complemented by a number of external organizations for specific tasks;

- has a structure that is hard to understand for non-experts, as it is mostly 'invisible' for users (they only directly see the user interfaces, which are the mere 'outside' of information systems making up the CIS).

2.1.2 The need for structure

As we have seen in the previous subsection, information processing in most organizations is complex, often very complex. To keep this information processing manageable, structure is required. We need this structure for two complementary reasons.

The first reason is operations management. This actually means running your information processing on a day-to-day basis in an effective and efficient way. This only works well if it is clear which systems do exactly what, how and when they exchange information, how to handle exceptions (like errors), and who is responsible for what. To use our analogy with the building world: architecture here is like a floor plan to navigate in the best way through a complex building.

The second reason is change management. This means that structure is needed to organize the evolution of information processing in an organization. Organizations change on a continuous basis for several reasons – not in the least because their environment changes continuously. This means that their information processing has to change, i.e. evolve, as well to keep supporting the organization well. Architecture is the basis for managing this evolution: you cannot change a structure without properly understanding it. In our analogy with the building world: you cannot structurally change a building without knowing its structure[2]. We revisit this topic in Section 2.1.5, where we discuss system evolution, and Section 2.7, where we discuss architecture as a tool for achieving business agility.

The need for structure exists in all complex information processing situations but arises most clearly in two situations. The first is the situation where information processing has evolved over time without explicit structure and has resulted in a situation that has become unmanageable, the so-called *legacy problem*. The second is the situation where a new organization starts its information processing small and simple (and hence well-organized) but grows

---

[2] Strictly speaking, you can of course. But often this results in unusable buildings or even more badly, collapsing buildings. This is no different for the information systems domain. Information systems do not physically collapse when modified the wrong way, but just stop working properly. When they stop working properly, they may start producing wrong results or taking wrong actions – which may go unnoticed for a while, with all problematic consequences.

without adapting it. This is the situation that we call the *greenfield problem*. We discuss both situations in the next subsections.

2.1.3 The legacy problem

When designing the structure of a CIS, one most often does not start from scratch. Starting from scratch (indicated as a *greenfield* situation, which we discuss in the next subsection) typically only happens in the case of a completely new organization. In an existing organization, we find a CIS with an existing structure (referred to as a *brownfield* situation).

The overall structure of such an existing CIS is typically historically grown in the organization. Through a long history of (often ad-hoc) changes, the structure may have evolved into something rather 'unstructured': though every system obviously has *a* structure, this structure may be very inadequate for maintaining the system. Typical problems are many ad-hoc dependencies between parts of the system, partly replicated functionality in the system, replicated (and possibly inconsistent) data in the system, inconsistent use of underlying technology, etcetera. The documentation of the structure of the CIS and of the structure of its component information systems is often of a poor nature – or even completely missing. Sometimes the source code (i.e., the specification of the system in some programming language) is considered to be the documentation[3].

Making major changes to a CIS (like replacing a component IS) is therefore a formidable task that can take years of time and millions of Euros or Dollars of investment. It can be compared to adding a new subway line in a major metropolis (often without having proper maps outlining all the surface and underground infrastructures). When extending a subway, the overall system cannot be halted during the construction, as this would paralyze the metropolis. Likewise, major changes to a CIS must be performed without halting the CIS for a substantial time, as this would also halt the operation of the organization that is served by the CIS – note that almost any modern large organization is heavily dependent on its information systems[4]. And there is a snake in the grass: whereas the complexity of a subway system in a metropolis is evident (you can go to see, touch and experience it), the complexity of a CIS is hidden to its users: it is 'in the box' (or 'behind the screen'). Therefore, it may be much harder to justify any disruptions caused by changing a CIS – or explain why changes need to be waited for.

---

[3] Using the source code of a complex information system as documentation is about as effective as documenting the structure of a large building by means of specifying its individual bricks.

[4] Modern economists consider information the fourth basic production factor, next to the traditional triplet capital, labor force and raw materials (or the fifth, if you count land as the fourth – depending on which model you prefer).

2.1.4 The greenfield problem

As we have discussed above, business information system engineering typically takes place in an existing, complex context that may be dominated by legacy issues (the *brownfield* situation). These legacy issues complicate the evolution of complex information systems to desired, well-structured situations. In *greenfield* situations, we do not have these legacy problems: we can start from scratch. But this does not mean that there are no potential problems.

Greenfield situations typically exist with new organizations. Most new organizations are small in size and have relatively simple formal business processes. In terms of the organization classification of Mintzberg [Min83], they often have the simple structure or the adhocracy structure. This means that their business information processing requirements are often relatively simple too. Consequently, they can do with relatively simple automated solutions in terms of business information systems.

When these organizations are successful and grow, their business information processing requirements grow as well. This means that at some point (when the organization gets a more complex structure like a professional bureaucracy or a machine bureaucracy), the necessity emerges to move from systems for small organizations to systems for large organizations. This is, however, not as simple as just buying new systems: data has to be migrated between systems, business processes may have to be adapted, and staff may need to be trained or hired for the new systems.

The resulting potential problem is the greenfield problem: a growing organization can wait too long with rightsizing its business information systems structure, and hence can be hindered in its growth by 'too small' systems, and may start working around this situation, creating what can be considered a 'fresh' legacy problem.

2.1.5 Extending and restraining information systems

Information systems do not exist in a static environment. They typically exist in an environment where requirements to their functionality evolve continuously (often in an increasing fashion, i.e., the systems should be able to provide more functionality). They also exist in an environment where supporting technology continuously evolves, hence providing a stronger basis for the realization of the systems. These two perspectives of the environment are shown in Figure 3. Both environments increase the complexity of information systems, as illustrated by the large upward vertical arrows.

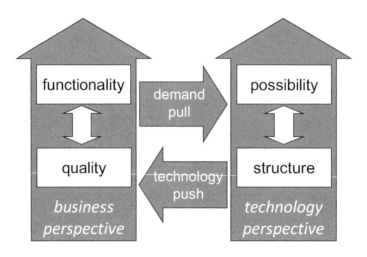

Figure 3: forces in information system development (adapted from [Gre03])

On the left-hand side of the figure, we see that increasing functionality can lead to a tension field with required quality (illustrated by the small vertical arrow): 'more' does not always imply 'better' – certainly not if development efforts are limited. This is the *demand pull* side (also called *requirements pull* side) of information system development with its associated problems. On the right-hand side of the figure, we see that increasing the use of the possibilities of technologies can lead to a challenged structure: too many connected technologies with consequently many interfaces can lead to unclear system structures. This is the *technology push* side of information system development with its associated problems. As illustrated by the two horizontal arrows in the figure, the demand pull and technology push forces reinforce each other: more requirements lead to the development and application of new technology, more technology leads to the discovery and demand of new possible functionalities.

The discussed forces lead to a situation where one needs a balance between extending information systems to match new requirements and technologies on the one hand, and proper quality and structure on the other hand. This is exactly where architecture comes in: it is a main approach for the balancing act. In software engineering, the balancing situation has long ago been recognized in wat is known as Lehman's laws of software evolution [Leh80], which describe a balance between forces driving new developments on one hand, and forces that slow down progress on the other hand [Wi24f].

2.2 The two faces of architecture

To deal with the complex situation outlined above, the concept of *architecture* has emerged in the information system field during the past decades.

The use of architecture aims at bringing structure into the design of complex business information systems. The term 'design' can be interpreted in two ways here:

- design related to the structure of a *product* (an information system being made), or

- design related to the structure of a *process* (the way of making an information system).

These two faces are both represented in the existing theory on business information system architecture (and enterprise architecture – we will explain the difference in the sequel of this chapter).

The product-oriented face of architecture focuses on architectures as sets of structural blueprints for the realization of information systems. This is very much like the use of blueprints for the realization of other complex artifacts, such as buildings or automobiles. In this face of architecture, the focus is on techniques for the structured specification of architectures, rules for the relationships between models produced (like consistency rules), and blueprints (or other indications) for how to produce the models (for the description of which we need the process-oriented face of architecture). The techniques are usually mainly of a graphical character, again much like the blueprints for other types of artifacts.

The process-oriented face of architecture focuses on procedural prescriptions for the realization of information systems. These prescriptions can have the form of methods, approaches or guidelines. Modeling methods provide formal or semi-formal, structured approaches consisting of well-described design steps and an indication of the artifacts they produce (for the description of which we need the product-oriented face of architecture). Modeling approaches are general, high-level descriptions of how to perform the architecting process. Modeling guidelines are typically more or less informal statements about architecture processes, for example based on best practices.

Both faces of architecture are (obviously) interrelated. Some of the relationships between the two faces as described above are shown in Figure 4. The arrows in this figure show how elements refer to each other. For example, modeling methods can refer to specification techniques by indicating which techniques are to be used in which steps of a method. Note that there are (again obviously) also relationships between elements within the same face of architecture. For example, a modeling approach may refer to the application of specific modeling guidelines.

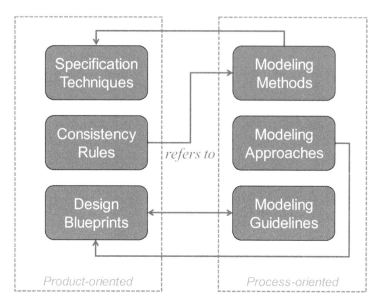

Figure 4: the two faces of architecture with some of their relations

Sets of architecture principles exist that have the character of guidelines, but which may refer to both the product- and the process-oriented face of architecture. An example is provided in [Gre11], where the majority of principles refer to the product-oriented face (for example "applications are modular") and a number refer to the process-oriented face (for example "application development is standardized"). We revisit this example in Section 5.5.

In this book, we take the product-oriented face of architecture as a starting point and step to the process-oriented face where appropriate (for example, Chapter 5 is completely based on the process-oriented face). We start the product-oriented exploration in the section below.

2.3 Architecture as a structural blueprint

An architecture of an information system (or a CIS) can be seen as the high-level blueprint of that system that serves to understand its internal structure to aid in its design, redesign, configuration and maintenance – not so much different from the (technical) architecture of a complex building or a subway system. We now define the concept of architecture, starting with software architectures and then moving on to information system architectures.

2.3.1 Architecture of a software system

The concept of architecture of software systems partly originates from the domain of software engineering, i.e., the field in which the detailed structuring of computer programs is the focus. The following is a definition of the term architecture from a well-known book that is considered a basic work in the domain of software architecture [Sha96]:

> *The architecture of a software system defines that system in terms of computational components and interactions between those components.*

The *computational components* form the *functional units* of a system, i.e., the parts that each provides something of the overall functionality. The term *computational* refers to the computations that a computer must make to realize the functionality. The *interactions* between the components allow them to operate as a whole to achieve the desired functionality of the software system.

The IEEE defines architecture as follows in its 1471 standard [Mai01, Hil07], including the environment of a system and the design principles used to obtain and maintain the structure of a system:

> *Architecture is the fundamental organization of a system embodied in its components, their relationships to each other and to the environment and the principles guiding its design and evolution.*

The relationships between the components and to the environment are the *connectors* or *interfaces*, which describe how the functional units interact (as stated in the first definition above) to achieve the overall behavior of the system, for example by exchanging information.

In modern views on software development, architecture is seen as an (or even *the*) essential element to manage development and maintenance of complex software [Mar18]:

> *If architecture comes last, then the software system will become ever more costly to develop, and eventually change will become practically impossible for part or all of the system.*

2.3.2 Architecture of a (corporate) information system

In this book, we are interested in the structure of corporate information systems. This means that we don't look at small details of computer programs, but at much larger structures of complex systems. To support development and maintenance of corporate information systems, attention to architecture is at least as important as in the case of software engineering as discussed above.

The complexity of corporate information systems implies that we have to focus on specific aspects of the system, that we have to distinguish between multiple levels of the system, and that we need structuring principles to understand and manage this complexity (like the principles in the IEEE definition cited above). Hence, we use the following definition of the term architecture in this book[5]:

> *The architecture of a (corporate) information system defines that system in terms of functional components and relations between those components, from the viewpoint of specific aspects of that system, possibly organized into multiple levels, and based on specific structuring principles.*

The concepts of *aspects* and *levels* are elaborated in Chapter 3 – here we will see that there are multiple aspects and multiple dimensions that can be used to define levels in an architecture specification. Depending on the chosen aspect(s), *functional components* can be of different natures: for example, they can be components that perform business functions (software components), components that hold business data (data storage components), or (parts of) business processes. Likewise, *relations* between components can be of different natures too: for example, they can be interfaces between software components or references between data storage components. This will become more concrete in the sequel of this book. Structuring principles for architectures are discussed in Chapter 4 .

2.4   Architecture more precisely

So, what is an architecture precisely, concretely spoken? We can view an architecture from the perspectives of modeling theory and systems theory. We discuss both perspectives below.

2.4.1 Architecture as a set of models

In modeling theory, an architecture (specification) can be seen as a set of models of a CIS, typically complemented by textual descriptions (e.g., explanations or further details of the models and stating the structuring principles used in their design). Each model is a specific abstraction of a

---

[5] Note that the term 'architecture' is in general overloaded, as it can refer to a set of design principles (a set of norms or rules), to the process of applying these design principles (a process), and to the result of the application of design principles (a product). In our definition of the term 'architecture' and hence in the remainder of this book, we focus on the product interpretation, with proper attention for the relevance of the rules and process aspects. Other authors may take different positions, e.g. [Die08] focuses on the rules interpretation.

concrete information system. As such, a model can describe a functional component of a (part of a) CIS or an aspect of a (part of a) CIS.

Mathematically, we can put this as follows:

$$a(c) = \{m_1(c), m_2(c), \ldots, m_n(c)\}$$

where a is an architecture of a CIS c and each m_i is a model of c. The set of models together forms the architecture. We will revisit this mathematical view in Chapter 3 when we get to 'dissecting' an architecture into multiple models.

This information system described by an architecture may exist, in which case the models can be considered to be *descriptive*. The architecture may be the basis for an information system to be built yet, in which case the models can be considered to be *prescriptive'*.

The models are often of a graphical nature, but they may also (partly) be in textual or mathematical form (specifications).

The models are organized following the aspects and levels mentioned in the definition above. This means that each model is at a specific level in each dimension and covers one or more aspects. In the remainder of this book, we will see examples of these models.

2.4.2 Architecture as a system

From a system theory point of view, an architecture is a specification of a system. This system can be composed of *subsystems* and *aspect systems*.

Subsystems form a *structural decomposition* of a system: a set of sub-systems together form the super-system. Subsystems form a *partition* of a system: every element of the super-system is part of exactly one subsystem (this means that nothing is forgotten or replicated). To illustrate the concept, one can think of partitioning a house into multiple rooms: the house is the super-system formed by the combination of the rooms which are the subsystems. We will see in Section 3.3 that decomposition into sub-systems is a powerful way to deal with the complexity of architectures.

Aspect systems form a *characteristics decomposition* of a system: a set of aspect systems together describe the behavior of a system. The set of aspects provides a separation of concerns: we can look at each aspect of a system individually. To illustrate this concept, one can think of the exterior design of a house versus the interior design: they are two aspects that describe characteristics of the same house, yet different aspects. We will see in Section 3.2 that working with aspects is also a powerful way to deal with the complexity of architectures.

2.5 Other types of architectures

The concept of architecture has existed for long in other domains, most notably the domain of designing buildings. Below, we first discuss similarities and differences between architecture in the IS and building domain. Next, we look at other uses of the architecture concept in the computer science domain.

2.5.1 Architecture in building

Architecture in the building domain has existed for several millennia now. Even the old Egyptians used to be architecture masters – the results of which we can still observe in the form of their pyramids and temples. The same goes for the ancient Greek and the Romans (e.g., the architect Vitruvius, who defined a set of architectural criteria [Wi24b]). The tradition of architecting has continued into the modern time, resulting in many architecture styles.

There are many parallels between traditional building and IS in the use of the architecture concept [Tay10]. In the building domain, an architecture too is a high-level blueprint of an artifact (in this case a building) that shows how its elements are interconnected or composed (see e.g. [Chi96, Han09]). It can have various aspects, like frontal view, top view, interior view, or technical view – we will see in Chapter 3 how this is also the case for IS architectures. Complex buildings can be described at several levels, where the highest level shows the overall structure of the building and the lowest level goes into the structure of smaller parts (e.g., individual rooms) – again, we will see in Chapter 3 how this also applies to IS architectures. And building architectures are usually structured according to well-known principles too (that is why we are seldom completely lost in a building). We use these parallels between the building world and the information system world throughout this book to create an intuitive understanding and feeling for information system architectures. But there are also some important differences between the two fields that we should understand [Tay10] – we discuss several important differences below.

Firstly, buildings and information systems are very different things, reflecting on the nature of architectures designed for them. Buildings are physical, whereas information systems consist of intangible software. Buildings are subjected to physical laws of nature (like gravity), information systems are not[6].

---

[6] This is one of the reasons why the 'size' of buildings (interpreted as their physical height) increases only slowly over time (see for example the development of the height of sky scrapers [Woo15]), whereas the 'size' of software systems (interpreted as the size of their executable code) can easily 'explode' in a relatively short period. Note that in the eighties, software was often distributed on floppy disks (with a size of no more than a few megabytes), then in the nineties and the early twenty-first century on CDs or DVDs (with a size of many megabytes), and nowadays usually via online channels (with a size of often several gigabytes). Just imagine how large buildings would be if they would have 'grown' at the same rate.

People have very well-established experience with the use of buildings, often far less with the use of information systems. Software can be easily copied and transported, buildings obviously cannot.

Secondly, architecture in the building domain has existed for a few millennia (see for example Figure 5), whereas architecture in the IS domain has existed only for a few decades. The building domain has a well-established basis and a set of well-accepted principles. For example, the tasks and responsibilities of architects in practice have been described in great detail [Cha10]. The building domain also has a huge historical showcase [Pal08], even with books specializing on showcases, e.g., [Unw10], which describes a set of buildings that "every architect should understand". Architecture in the IS domain, however, is still much in its infancy. We are still in the era of discovering 'how it all works' in practice. Our intuition for the IS domain is not nearly as well developed as for the building domain and hence we must be more methodical and analytical in our approach to information system architecture design [Tay10].

Figure 5: an example of ancient Greek architecture (source unknown)

Thirdly, software is much more malleable than physical building materials, offering possibilities for changes – both in terms of types of changes and frequency of changes – to constructs that are unthinkable in the building domain [Tay10]. Hence, information systems (and their descriptive architectures) can be changed in ways that are impossible for physical buildings (and their descriptive architectures). For example, in a complex information system with a well-designed architecture, it may be well possible to insert an additional module to extend the central functionality. Inserting an additional middle floor in an existing high-rise building is a bit more of a problem. The fact that software is

17

more malleable than physical materials can in fact also be a problem, as it opens the opportunity to continuously change things in a 'quick-and-dirty' way, leading to chaotically organized information systems (which are often the cause of the legacy problem that we discuss in Section 2.1.2).

Fourthly, the aesthetics aspect is very important in the building domain (e.g., many people appreciate symmetry in buildings), for the simple reason that buildings are very visible artifacts[7]. We show a nice example (at least, to the taste of the author of this book) of modern building architecture in Figure 6. Obviously, the aesthetic aspect plays a major role here. There are even books primarily focusing on the outside of buildings [Faj08]. Information systems, on the other hand, mainly consist of software that is 'invisible': although the software controls the behavior of devices (like screens or printers), the software itself is hidden 'inside the machine' once it is used. Aesthetics does play an indirect role in IS architecture, however, because architecture is about models, and aesthetic models are often good models [Gre03] (or maybe the other way around: if models are really ugly, it is often an indication of their poor quality).

Figure 6: modern architecture applied in building: top station of the Hungerburgbahn in Innsbruck, Austria, designed by Zaha Hadid (photo by author)

---

[7] If we take the importance of aesthetics in building architecture to the extreme, we can quote the words of the famous architect Philip Johnson from 1964: "Architecture is the art of how to waste space."

Fifthly, digital information technology has developed much faster than building technology across its development lifespan of less than a century – and is still developing at a sometimes dizzying speed. Take for example a state-of-the-art, enterprise-level storage system from the early days of the information systems history: the IBM 305 RAMAC was an advanced storage system in 1956 (shown in Figure 7). It had a (for those days) whopping storage capacity of 4.4 MB (yes, megabytes) for the price of a very, very nice villa. At the time of writing this book, a micro-SD card the size of a small fingernail has a storage capacity of 1 TB for the price of a pair of trousers[8]. The increase in storage capacity is enormous. Compare this to the increase of storage capacity (or height, or any other measure that you like) of buildings in the same period and you will find much, much smaller numbers there. As a consequence, the adequate and well-structured application of information technology can sometimes hardly keep up with the development of the technology. The technology push force of Figure 3 may confuse even information system designers.

Figure 7: IBM RAMAC 305 System (photo via Norsk Teknisk Museum)

2.5.2 Architecture in computer science

The concept of architecture is used in various sub-disciplines of computer science – where it always has the meaning of 'structural blueprint'. Without the

---

[8] This means an increase of storage capacity per device of about a factor 200,000. The factor becomes almost unimaginably large when you compute the increase of storage capacity per cost (e.g., per Euro) or even per volume (e.g., per cubic meter) – have fun and try and do the math!

aim of being complete, we may even depict a spectrum from 'very hard' to 'very soft' computer science:

VLSI architecture: VLSI (Very Large Scale Integration) is the term for complex computer chips, such as processor chips or memory chips. The term architecture is used to describe the electronic structure of these chips [Kae14]: one speaks for example about a 'processor architecture' (or 'processor microarchitecture'). Here the architecture elements are basic digital elements (such as digital logic ports), the relations are the electrical paths between the elements.

Computer architecture: The term 'computer architecture' [Led22] is used to describe the abstract structure of computer systems, such as PCs, laptops, or file servers. Nowadays, this term is also applicable to smartphones and tablets. Chips and basic devices are the elements in computer architecture, the relations again electrical connections, but now of a digital kind (e.g. busses). Computer architecture is mainly about hardware, although low-level software may play a role (like hardware drivers, operating system).

Software architecture: Software architecture [Sha96, Bas03] is concerned with the structure of complex computer programs (software), such as operating systems or application systems. The term is used in the field of software engineering. Elements in software architecture are programming language primitives, such as control statements (loops, choices), and structures such as functions, methods, modules.

IS architecture: As discussed before, IS architectures deal with the structure of complete information systems. Elements are mainly software modules (which can be described by software architectures[9]), but elements from the software context may be taken into account too, like elements from the (business) organization the software is embedded in.

CIS architecture: CIS architectures describe the structure of complete corporate information systems or inter-organizational information systems (e.g. used in e-business). The difference with IS architectures is determined by the aggregation scope: the elements in CIS architectures are information systems (which can each be described by an IS architecture).

VLSI and computer architecture are quite different from the other three types of architecture, as they mainly deal with hardware instead of software (taking into account all kinds of physical limitations, for example)[10]. Software architecture

---

[9] So one could view an information system architecture as a 'high-level' software architecture. Note that there is no strict boundary between software architecture and information system architecture when it comes to the 'size' of the software system it describes.

[10] When realizing information systems based on (C)IS architecture, these systems are deployed on computer systems based on computer architecture - so in this respect, the two types of architecture have an indirect relation in practice. In our view, (C)IS

has a number of things in common with C(IS) architecture but deals with a lower aggregation (and abstraction) level and hence can pay attention to smaller details and can use techniques not usable at the C(IS) level (like formal verification tools). The problems encountered in IS and CIS architecture are much alike, the main difference being the 'size' (and hence complexity) of the systems described[11]. This is the reason for the fact that we often treat both types of architectures in one go in this book.

2.5.3 Enterprise architecture

Enterprise architecture is a concept that is related to CIS architecture, but of a broader nature. In enterprise architecture, the structure of an entire organization (enterprise) is designed, usually with a focus on its information processing. In enterprise architecture, the structure of an organization includes:

- its organization structure, for example in terms of departments and roles of people within these departments;

- its business processes (or workflows), i.e., the flow of steps used in the organization to achieve specific business goals;

- the business functions used in the business processes;

- the structure of the information used in the business functions.

If we see enterprise architecture and CIS architecture as two different concepts, enterprise architecture can form a context for CIS architecture: it defines the context in which a CIS must operate. If we see enterprise architecture and CIS architecture as two concepts that share the common basis of structuring of information processing, but differ in their scope, we can see enterprise architecture as a 'broadened version' of CIS architecture (expanded with organizational aspects). Following the same line of reasoning, we can see software architecture as a 'narrowed version' of CIS architecture (restricted to pure software aspects only). This line of reasoning is illustrated in Figure 8 as a spectrum of architecture types. We will see in the remainder of this book that CIS architecture is sometimes interpreted a bit more narrowly (moved to the left in the spectrum), sometimes a bit more broadly (moved to the right in the spectrum). CIS architecture design is (certainly in practice) not mathematically delineated engineering - which is not a problem when we make our architecting choices explicit and take their consequences fully into account.

---

architecture does not 'contain' computer architecture (and certainly not VLSI architecture). We revisit this issue in Section 3.6.2.

[11] Again, there is no strict boundary between the size of an IS and a CIS – this is heavily context-dependent. Typically, an IS supports a specific business function, whereas a CIS supports a complete organization (or a substantial part of it).

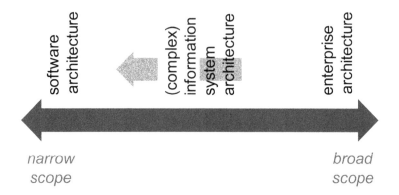

Figure 8: software, CIS and enterprise architecture as a spectrum

We discuss an example of an enterprise architecture framework in Section 5.1. An elaborate discussion of principles for enterprise architecture can be found in [Gre11] (discussed in Section 5.5 of this book).

2.6 The IS architect

In many large information-intensive organizations, the IS architect is seen as a separate profession. The IS architect is either employed within the organization or hired from a specialized consultancy organization.

Depending on the size of the organization, there may be a few architects employed, or there may be large teams. In the latter case, we often see specialization of architects that distinguishes several groups with dedicated attention. An import distinction is between architects that focus on business-related software (application architects) and architects that focus on supporting software (infrastructure architects) – in Chapter 6 of this book, we further elaborate this distinction.

The IS architect has a number of tasks; he or she

- analyzes, understands and organizes requirements (functional and nonfunctional) of stakeholders (like end users, managers, or investors);

- judges how well these requirements can indeed be matched by systems given the current technological state of the art;

- places requirements in the context of the functionality of existing information systems[12];

---

[12] This can be a hard job when dealing with old information systems with poor documentation, the so-called *legacy systems* – see our discussion in Section 2.1.

- designs abstract structures (architectures) of complex software systems, i.e., (corporate) information systems that implement the requirements;

- instructs software engineering departments for realizing these systems;

- oversees the entire realization process and communicates between stakeholders in the process from start of design to end of organizational implementation.

The above list implies that an architect needs to oversee several very different groups of stakeholders and communicate between them. This is illustrated in Figure 9 for an information system development project. Here the stakeholders range from the project principal (the 'owner' of the project that formally requests the execution of the project) to the software (and sometimes hardware) engineers that realize the system.

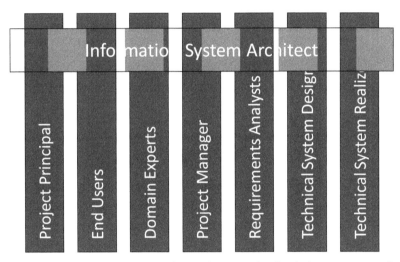

Figure 9: the architect overseeing and communicating between groups of stakeholders in an IS development project

The architect is thus a modeler, an engineer, a translator and a communicator[13]. This means that a good architect must combine the skills of a high-level engineer and those of a project manager. And sometimes he or she needs to be a bit of an artist too, given the state of infancy of the IS architecture domain.

Note that the role of an architect is essentially different from the role of a contractor: the latter oversees the realization of information systems the specifications of which have been created by an architect (quite comparable to the traditional building world). In terms of Figure 9, the contractor is mainly concerned with the two right-most groups of stakeholders. The role of contractor is especially important in situations where design and realization of

---

[13] See e.g. [Wie08] for an investigation into the required competences of IT architects.

an IS are heavily decoupled, e.g., in situations where software development is outsourced to a different country (also referred to as *offshoring*).

2.7 Architecture as a business agility instrument

In this chapter so far, we have described architecture as an instrument to deal with the complexity of information systems. As such, information systems architecture is a tool to enable information management and through this business operations management in an organization. Good information system architecture is thus essential for effective and efficient business management in almost any modern organization. This is reflected in the observation that modern economies not only rely on the three traditional production factors capital, materials and work force, but also (and often foremost) on information as the fourth production factor.

But apart from being effective and efficient, modern (business) organizations must also be agile: they must be able to quickly react (or even pro-act) to changes in their environment: new competitors, new product requirements, new customer groups, new legislation, et cetera. As organizations heavily rely on the functionality of their information systems, this implies that these information systems must be agile as well: they must be able to evolve swiftly with requirements of the organization they support (and its context). In other words, information system design must be responsive to the force of requirements pull.

Apart from requirements pull, there is also technology push: modern organization must be able to deploy modern information technology quickly to be able to participate in technology-driven markets. The most prominent example if of course the rise of the Internet and the Web, but other examples are the use of tagging technology like RFID (enabling the Internet of Things or IoT), the use of mobile technology, and the wide-spread use of artificial intelligence (AI). In other words: information system design must be responsive to the force of technology push.

As illustrated in Figure 10, the forces of requirements pull and technology push reinforce each other in driving the evolution of information systems, further increasing the need for agility.

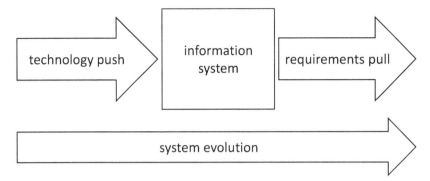

Figure 10: technology push and requirements pull forces in system evolution

Architecture plays a central role in allowing agility of information systems with respect to requirements pull and technology push: architecture can be seen as a pivot between business and organization structures on the one hand and technology on the other hand. This is shown in Figure 11, which illustrates how the business and organization side can move without affecting the technology side, and vice versa.

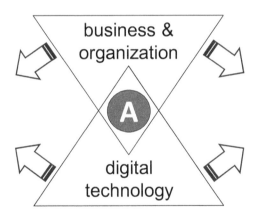

Figure 11: architecture (A) as a pivot between business and organization on the one hand, and technology on the other hand (adapted from [Gre16])

A well-designed architecture of an information system supports agility of that system in the following ways:

- The architecture is a conceptual specification of the structure of the system, such that redesign decisions of the system can be made on the basis of this specification, without taking irrelevant context and technical details into account. This is strongly related to the notion on *abstraction*, which we discuss in the next chapter.

- The architecture provides a clear modularization of the system, such that required changes can often be allocated to a specific module (or a small number of specific modules) of the system without affecting the other modules. In other words: local changes in business requirements lead to local changes in information systems.

- If changes cannot be contained in a specific module (locality as mentioned before cannot be kept), the architecture specifies all relevant dependencies between modules (and aspects) of the system, such that 'cascading changes' can easily be identified. In other words: a good architecture design clearly shows all 'indirect' changes required.

- The information system architecture as a model is a means of effective communication between the various stakeholders in a redesign project of the system (as shown in Figure 9), such that agreements between various stakeholders in that redesign project can be reached swiftly and clearly.

To arrive at well-designed architectures of information systems, we must first understand the dimensions along which we can design these architectures. These are the topic of the next chapter of this book.

3

UNDERSTANDING ARCHITECTURES IN DIMENSIONS

Architectures of large, complex business information systems are complex themselves too. As we have seen in the previous chapter (see Section 2.4.1), an information system architecture consists of a set of models. For large information systems (such as corporate information systems), this can be a large set of models – possibly in the order of thousands of models.

To understand these complex information system architectures, it is necessary to be able to look at these architectures in a well-structured way, i.e., using a well-structured framework. Without a framework, it is hardly possible to completely understand the relations between the constituent models of an architecture and thereby analyze its overall structure. Without a framework, it is also hardly possible too to compare two architectures in a well-structured way. And it is surely hardly possible to properly design complex, multi-model architectures without the structure of a framework.

This chapter introduces a framework for structuring complex, multi-model architectures. In the first section below, we introduce a set of four dimensions that we use to describe the characteristics of architecture models. In the next four sections, we elaborate each of these dimensions. In the last section of this chapter, we combine the four dimensions into an architecture 'analysis space'.

3.1 A set of architecture dimensions

To organize architecture descriptions in a structured way, we can distinguish various dimensions in a complex architecture description that consists of multiple individual models (remember the discussion of an architecture as a set of models in Section 2.4.1). These dimensions help us in making appropriate choices with respect to looking at architectures and describing them. We distinguish four dimensions in this book:

The aspect dimension describes a number of 'content' aspects from which we can view an architecture, providing a certain 'cross-section' of an entire architecture description.

The aggregation dimension describes the levels of aggregation, which determine the level of detail of an architecture description – ranging from very coarse (few large elements) to very detailed (many small elements).

The abstraction dimension describes the abstraction levels at which we describe an architecture, ranging from very abstract (i.e., few concrete choices have been made regarding the elements in the architecture) to very concrete (i.e., all concrete choices have been made).

The realization dimension describes the spectrum from very business-oriented descriptions (in terms of business requirements with no attention for IT elements) to very IT-oriented descriptions (in terms of technical systems with no attention for business elements).

The first dimension is about the 'aspects' in our definition of architecture (see Section 2.3). The other three dimensions are about the 'levels' in this definition. Note that the first three dimensions describe 'time-independent' characteristics of architecture descriptions, whereas the realization dimension describes characteristics related to 'phases' in de development of an architecture description. As such, one could argue that this dimension describes a context of architecture development (as in enterprise architecture, see Section 2.5) instead of architecture itself. We treat it as part of an architecture in this book, however, as it does highlight the business and technical context of architecture design and analysis.

Note that our choice of dimensions is not the only possible choice: there are many more possibilities. For example, in [Gre11], a set of ten (nine plus one) dimensions is discussed. Our set of four dimensions can be mapped to a subset of these ten dimensions (be it not strictly one-to-one).

In the four sections below, we discuss each of the four dimensions we have chosen in more detail. The dimensions are to a large extent orthogonal, i.e., choices in various dimensions can be more or less freely combined. How to make combinations is discussed in the sixth and last section of this chapter.

3.2 Aspect dimension

In this section, we explore the aspect dimension of information systems architecture. We first discuss the notion of 'aspect'. Then, we discuss two specific example aspect frameworks: one designed by Jan Truijens (and its modernized version), and one designed by Philippe Kruchten. These are example frameworks as other frameworks exist. Finally, we show how the frameworks of Truijens and Kruchten can be compared.

3.2.1 The notion of aspect

An aspect of an information system architecture is a specific way to look at that architecture by focusing on specific characteristics of that architecture only. One single architecture can be looked at from different aspects, e.g. by focusing on software structures only or focusing on data structures only. As an architecture is a set of models, an aspect is defined by choosing models with the right modeling abstractions. In other words, an aspect defines which characteristics are included in the models under consideration and thus which are left out. All models of an architecture in a specific aspect form an aspect architecture.

The notion of aspect is well known in the world of building architectures. In the architecture of a house, for example, one can distinguish between the external architecture, the interior architecture, and the infrastructure architecture. The external architecture focuses on the externally visible structure of the house – possibly even distinguishing between the aspects front view, side view and rear view. The internal architecture describes the same house but focuses on the organizations of the rooms on the inside of the house. The infrastructure architecture describes the same house again but describes how the plumbing and electricity circuitry is organized in the house. One reason for having multiple aspects is to avoid too complex descriptions (having all in one diagram may be quite confusing). A second reason is the fact that not everybody is interested in all aspects. A furniture designer, for example, will be interested in the interior architecture and maybe even in the exterior architecture, but hardly in the plumbing of the house. The situation with information system architectures is quite analogous.

Below, we discuss two examples of concrete aspect frameworks: the one by Truijens and the one by Kruchten. Note that there are other aspect frameworks; in software engineering, for example, often the aspects *function*, *behavior* and *data* are distinguished.

3.2.2 The Truijens 5 aspects framework

Quite some time ago already, Truijens described an aspect framework for information systems with five aspects [Tru90]. The five aspects of this framework are the following (see also Figure 12):

The data aspect describes the organization of the data in an information system, typically in terms of data structure diagrams or specifications.

The system aspect specifies the structure of the software of the information system under consideration, i.e., the system that is being designed or analyzed. This can also be referred to as the *application logic structure*.

The configuration aspect describes the structure of the platform used by the information system under consideration, i.e., the software (and possibly hardware) that the application logic relies on. Examples here are operating systems and database systems.

The communication aspect specifies how the information system communicates with other information systems by defining the communication topologies, the messages passed and possibly the protocols used for message passing.

The organization aspect finally describes how the information system under consideration is embedded into an organization for its design, implementation and maintenance.

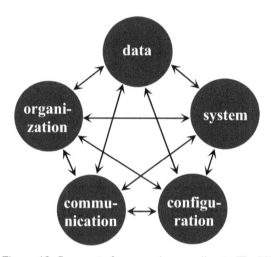

Figure 12: 5 aspects framework according to [Tru90]

As shown in the figure by the arrows, these five aspects are all interrelated: decisions in one aspect influence decisions in another aspect. For example: if the data aspect architecture gets more complex, this may imply that the system aspect architecture gets more complex too as the software will require functionality to deal with the new data structures. Note that it is not always necessary to specify all aspects – this depends on the purpose of the architecture.

Each aspect of the framework requires its own specification technique for modeling. We discuss these techniques after we have discussed a modernized version of the framework in the next subsection.

As the Truijens framework covers more than software structures only (most clearly in the organization aspect), it contains elements of enterprise architecture. In terms of the discussion in Section 2.5.3, it is in the right half of the spectrum illustrated in Figure 8.

3.2.3 A modern variation on the Truijens framework

The framework of Truijens dates back a considerable time (in terms of insights in the development of information system architecture): it was published in 1990. The framework makes two assumptions that can be considered not quite contemporary anymore:

- It considers (business) data as an aspect but does not consider business processes as a separate aspect. This is probably due to the period of development of the framework, in which business process management was not yet considered a separate perspective on corporate information systems (business process support was embedded in application systems, belonging to the system aspect).
- It considers configuration and communication as two separate aspects, as computers and their interconnections were seen as two different matters in those days. Nowadays, all information systems are implicitly considered to be distributed, i.e., to include interconnections.

Based on the two above observations, we can construct a 'modernized' version of the framework of Truijens, in which the process aspect has been added, and in which the configuration and communication are merged into one aspect labeled 'platform'. The system aspect has been relabeled 'software' (with the term system made implicit) to stress the observation that 'system' in general is a broader term. The resulting framework is shown in Figure 13. It is referred to as the UT5 model (for Updated Truijens 5-aspect framework) [Gre21], an acronym that we also use in the rest of this book.

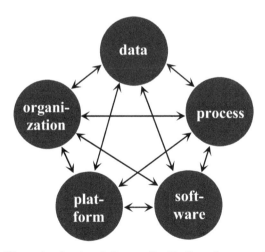

Figure 13: modernized variation on the Truijens framework (UT5)

The five aspects of the UT5 framework are described as follows:

The data aspect describes the organization of the data in an information system, typically in terms of data structure diagrams or specifications. The specification of the data aspect of an architecture is sometimes referred to as the *data architecture* [Kni14]. As such, a data architecture is part of an overall business information system architecture (or enterprise architecture), describing only the data aspect of it.

The process aspect describes the organization of the (business) processes managed by or executed in an information system, typically in terms of business process models. A structure for the specification of a set of processes is sometimes referred to as a *process architecture* [Mal14, Dij16]. As such, a process architecture is part of an overall business information system architecture (or enterprise architecture), describing only the process aspect of it.

The software aspect describes the organization of the software of an information system in terms of its modules and the connections between these modules. Comparably to the previous two aspects, the term *software architecture* [Sha96, Bas03, Tay10] is commonly used to describe the architecture that describes only the software aspect of an overall business information system architecture (or enterprise architecture).

The platform aspect describes the organization of the software and hardware underlying an information system, i.e., the information technology assumed to be present to use the information system, both in terms of computing and communication (networking) facilities. It can be considered the specification of the structure of the 'technical foundation' of the information system under consideration (analogous to the foundation under a building). In a design effort, the platform typically pre-exists or is bought – it is outside the scope of the design itself.

The organization aspect describes how the information system under consideration is embedded into an organization (in terms of organizational roles and functions) for its design, implementation and maintenance.

3.2.4 Specifying aspect architectures

Like in the original version of the Truijens framework, each aspect of the UT5 framework requires its own way of modeling and associated specification techniques. We discuss this below for the five aspects.

Data aspect

To model the data aspect, we typically create data models. We can use various techniques to describe data models, like the UML class modeling technique [Mil06] or the entity-relationship (ER) technique [Tha00]. A very simple example of a UML class model diagram for a club administration system is shown in Figure 14. In this model, we see the main data classes with their attributes, as well as the relations between the classes with their constraints. For example, the diagram states that a *Committee* consists of 5 or more *ClubMembers* and exactly one *Chairperson*. It also states that a *Legal Entity* must either be a *Person* or a *BusinessEntity* (never neither nor both).

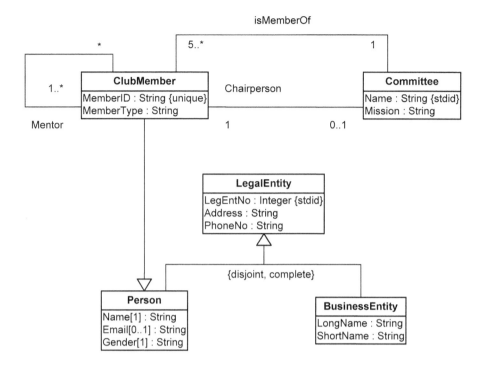

Figure 14: simple example of a UML class diagram
for the data architecture aspect ^(source unknown)

System aspect

To model the system aspect, we create software system models, for example using the UML component diagram technique [Mil06]. A very simple example of such a diagram is shown in Figure 15, showing the system aspect of the architecture of a financial information system. In this diagram, we see the main software building blocks (modules or subsystems) of the system, as well as the way these building blocks use the functionality of other blocks through interfaces. For example, the *Payment Checking* module uses the functionality of the *General Ledger* building block to enter payments into the bookkeeping of the organization using the system.

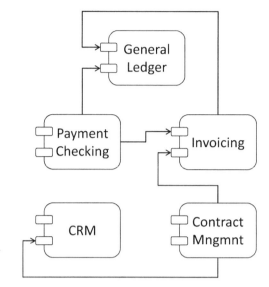

Figure 15: simple example of a UML component diagram
for the system architecture aspect

Alternatives to the UML component diagram technique are the SysML block definition diagram [Del13, Kau18] and (more traditionally) data flow diagrams [Gan79, Wi24i].

Process, organization and platform aspects

For the process aspect, we can use process model specification techniques like BPMN diagrams [Fre19] or UML activity diagrams [Pil05]. For the organization aspect, we can use techniques like organigrams (also referred to as organizational charts) [Wi24g]. For the platform aspect, technology stack models can be used (also referred to as solution stack models or software stack models) [Wi24h]. In the next subsection, we show a more elaborate set of example models, addressing all of the five aspects of the UT5 framework.

In the rest of this book, we use the UT5 aspect framework of Figure 13, as this model is more up-to-date than the original model of Figure 12.

3.2.5 Example application case of the UT5 framework

As an example of the use of the UT5 framework, we apply it in the world of smart manufacturing [Nag21] (also labeled as Industry 4.0 [GTI14]). We have chosen this example domain deliberately to illustrate that information system architecture also plays an important role in application domains other than the often shown administrative domain (as we have seen in the simple examples in Section 3.2.4).

In the world of manufacturing, we see an increasing application of digital technologies for the control of manufacturing processes and functions. This leads to increasingly complex manufacturing information systems, consisting of several individual systems that support specific aspects of manufacturing. Because of this, information system architecture is becoming increasingly important in the manufacturing domain.

In this section, we focus on the (simplified) architecture design of a manufacturing process control system (MPCS), in which a manufacturing process management system (MPMS) [HA16, Gre21, Tra21] is a major component. This MPCS manages the manufacturing processes in a factory, which also cover the physical processes that take place on the shop floor to create products. Below, we show a simple example aspect architecture model for each of the five aspects in the UT5 framework of Figure 13. Note that the full aspect architecture specifications in practice are much more complex.

Software aspect

The software aspect describes the structure of the application software, which can be described at various levels (we discuss this in Section 3.3, including a multi-level elaboration of the current example). At the highest level of the CIS software architecture, we present the MPCS in its system context: we see the systems in an information system landscape for manufacturing.

This landscape is shown as a software aspect architecture in Figure 16, using an informal notation[14] that can be read as a data flow diagram (DFD) [Gan79, Wi24i]. It contains an enterprise-level business process management system (BPMS), an enterprise resource planning (ERP) system, the MPCS, a manufacturing execution system (MES) and a product lifecycle management system (PLMS). In Section 3.3, we zoom in into the 'internals' of the MPCS.

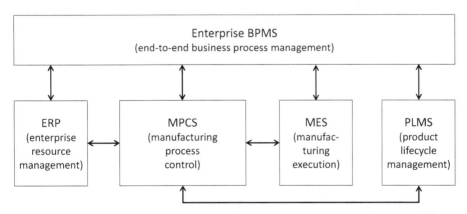

Figure 16: software aspect context architecture of example manufacturing CIS

---

[14] The landscape can as well be shown in the format of a UML component diagram as illustrated in the simple example of Figure 16.

Data aspect

The data aspect of the architecture describes the high-level data structures for the MPCS (so part of the data structures of the entire CIS of Figure 16, as the complete set of data structures is too large and complex to be presented here). A high-level view of these data structures in the form of a conceptual data model is shown in Figure 17. The figure uses the UML class diagram notation [Pil05, Wi24c].

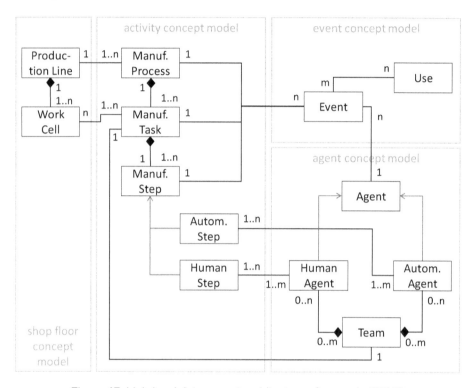

Figure 17: high-level data aspect architecture of example MPMS

In the figure, we see that the data elements in the structure are grouped into four clusters that respectively describe the data structures for specifying:

- shop floor structures, i.e., the physical organization of the work floor in a factory into production lines and work cells (in the left side of the figure);
- manufacturing activities (manufacturing tasks that consist of manufacturing steps) that make up the physical manufacturing processes in a factory (in the middle of the figure);
- the data structures for specifying manufacturing agents, i.e., the humans (human agents) and machines (automated agents, including industrial robots) that execute the manufacturing processes (in the bottom-right of the figure);

- the events that occur during manufacturing – used for example for exception management in the manufacturing process (in the top-right of the figure).

The four clusters are linked by relations, for example to specify that a *Manufacturing Task* is always executed in a *Work Cell*, or that a *Manufacturing Step* is always executed by an *Agent*, but we differentiate between human-operated steps and automated steps.

The conceptual data model is the basis for the design of the databases that will hold the actual operational data. The shown model can be further refined for this purpose [Gre21]. For example, the details of human and automated agents need to be further detailed to be able to assign the right agents to the right tasks.

Process aspect

The process aspect of the architecture describes the high-level structure of manufacturing processes that are supported by the manufacturing CIS. An overview of this is given in Figure 18 in the form of a business process model in BMPN notation [Fre19] with three swim lanes[15]. The process part supported by the MPCS (i.e., the actual physical manufacturing process) is related to the manufacturing department, which is shown in the bottom two swim lanes of Figure 18. As can be seen from the process model, this is a make-to-order process of standard products.

---

[15] In a BPMN diagram, swim lanes are generally used to divide a process specification into parts that are executed by different organizational entities. In Figure 18, swim lanes are used to (a) distinguish between the manufacturing department and other departments, and (b) to divide the manufacturing department into the design office (where products to manufacture are designed) and the shop floor (where the actual manufacturing of products takes place).

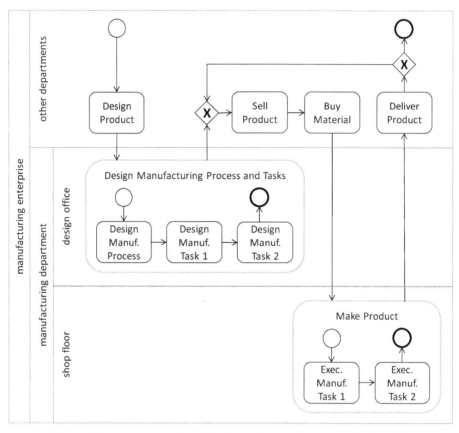

Figure 18: process aspect architecture of example manufacturing CIS

Obviously, the process model of Figure 18 can be further refined to show more detail. Also, it can be adapted to cover other production types, like design-to-order for customized products, or extended for hybrid manufacturing scenarios [Gre21].

Platform aspect

A high-level overview of the platform aspect architecture of the MPCS is shown in Figure 19. Here we see how the MPCS uses cyber-physical middleware[16] to connect to the physical manufacturing contexts (for example industrial robot control software), a database management system (DBMS) to store its data and share data with the enterprise context (as shown in Figure 16) and a standard business process management system (BPMS) to link manufacturing processes to enterprise-level processes (as shown in Figure 18). The other enterprise information systems (EIS) can use the MPCS.

---

[16] Middleware is software to connect systems. We explain this kind of software in detail in Chapter 9 of this book. Cyber-physical systems are systems that can deal both with aspects of the physical world and aspects of the digital world.

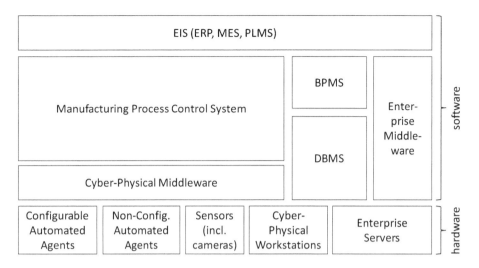

Figure 19: high-level platform aspect architecture of example manufacturing CIS

The figure shows that a platform aspect architecture can have multiple layers (shown as a vertical stack). In the figure, the EIS level is built on the underlying software layers, which in turn are built on the hardware layers. The shown platform architecture therefore is a layered architecture, following the layered architecture style that we address in Section 4.1.3.

In Figure 19, we see some components that are also present in the software aspect architecture of Figure 16. The platform architecture shows the 'stacking' of technologies (and the systems containing these technologies), the software architecture the interfaces between software components. This is an example of the interrelationship between aspect architectures, as indicated by the arrows in the UT5 framework (see Figure 13).

Organization aspect

Finally, the organization architecture of the MPCS in the context of the overall manufacturing CIS is shown in Figure 20. In this organogram we see the organization structure of the manufacturing environment (the grayed boxes) and the organization functions that are stakeholders in the processes relevant to the MPCS (the white boxes).

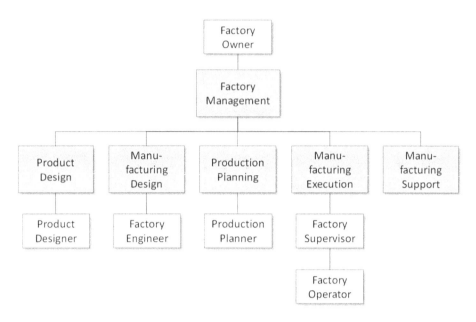

Figure 20: organization aspect architecture of example manufacturing CIS

3.2.6 The Kruchten 4+1 aspect framework

Philippe Kruchten has defined an aspect framework several decades ago that has become a standard in the world of software engineering and software architecture design. This framework has been the trigger for the definition of the IEEE Architecture Standard 1471 [Mai01, Hil07].

Kruchten's *4+1* framework [Kru95] (we abbreviate this to *K4+1*, analog to the *UT5* label introduced before) organizes the description of an architecture around four aspects, which are called *views* in the terminology of this framework. The use of views supports a well-defined separation of concerns in software development, based on the various groups of stakeholders that are involved in the development process. The four views of the K4+1 framework are the following (see Figure 21):

The logical view specifies the object/module models of the design, i.e., the structure of the application logic in abstract terms.

The development view specifies the organization of the software in a development environment, i.e., the way the software development is supported.

The process view specifies the concurrency and synchronization aspects of the software design, i.e., the way objects or modules in the logical view dynamically collaborate, possibly in parallel.

The physical view describes the mapping(s) of software onto hardware, thereby reflecting the distribution aspect (what runs where?).

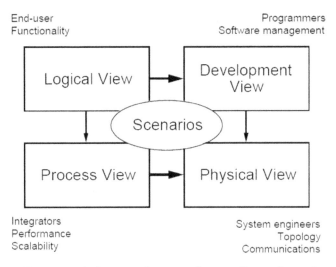

Figure 21: 4+1 aspect framework according to [Kru95]

Each view has its prime stake holder type and its major concerns, as shown in Figure 21. The *logical view* defines what the information system does, i.e., its functionality – clearly this is of prime interest to the end users of the system described by the architecture. The *development view* caters for the interests of the programmers and software managers that implement the system: it is about producing software. The *process view* addresses the system integrators that are interested in aspects like the performance and scalability of the system. Finally, the *physical view* describes the system in its execution environment, which is the domain of the system engineers.

The four views have a content dependency relationship, indicated by the arrows in the figure. The logical view is the basis for the development view and the process view. The physical view relies on information from both the development and the process views.

The four views as explained above are illustrated by the fifth element of the K4+1 framework:

The scenarios describe a few selected use cases that illustrate the four basic views. The scenarios make things concrete and provide a basis for discussions between the various groups of stake holders in the architecture design or analysis.

The purpose of the scenarios is to keep a software development and deployment project on a coherent path. This is often very necessary because the various stakeholders can think from very different perspectives and projects may take a long time to complete.

A very concrete example of the application of the Kruchten framework can be found in the system design process of the HORSE project [Gre21] that has realized the MPMS discussed in Section 3.2.5. In this European project, an

41

advanced manufacturing control system has been developed that supports the integration of flexible business process management and hybrid human-robotic manufacturing in a broad field of application scenarios. The complexity of the design of the HORSE system and the target of multiple application contexts very explicitly require a separation between the views in the framework. In the logical view, the architecture of the system is designed without taking specific technical choices for information technology into consideration, focusing on manufacturing functionality only. In the development and process views, these technical choices are made for the implementation of a software system that can be deployed in various manufacturing contexts. In the physical view, this software system can be tailored towards specific deployment contexts, such as a small manufacturing plant with relatively simple manufacturing processes or a large plant with complex processes.

3.2.7 UT5 versus K4+1

The obvious question now is how different aspect frameworks relate. Or to be more concrete: how do the UT5 and K4+1 frameworks relate? Doing some simple math, we easily find out that 4+1=5, so both frameworks have the same number of elements. Further, both are based on the 'separation of concerns' principle: focus on specific concerns in each aspect architecture, because the 'complete picture' is too complex.

The aspects in the respective frameworks are different however: they cannot be directly mapped one-to-one. They can be related to each other in some ways, though. For example:

- The system aspect of UT5 is comparable to the logical view of K4+1, be it that elements of the process view are included in the system aspect.

- The platform aspect of UT5 is related to the physical view of K4+1, as they both relate to execution environments for information systems – though their scopes are different.

Clearly, the fifth element of K4+1 is really different (this is why it is labeled as K4+1 instead of as K5) – it is not a view. It is a complement to the four views and hence has an integrative goal, whereas the other four are orthogonal. This fifth element is not included in the UT5 framework.

The two frameworks have emerged from slightly different architecture domains: the UT5 framework comes from information system engineering, the K4+1 framework from software engineering. These different originations account for some subtle differences in terminology and elements covered (see also the discussion in Section 2.5).

Finally, the K4+1 framework imposes a modeling order between its aspects (views), whereas the UT5 framework does not. As such, the K4+1 framework has elements of an *architecture design approach* whereas the UT5 framework may be considered a general *architecture design framework* (we discuss these concepts further in Chapter 5 of this book).

It is possible, however, to combine both frameworks in architecture development, where the K4+1 framework is used to describe views in terms of phasing in architecture development and the UT5 framework to describe aspects within (and across) these phases. This has been used for example in the mentioned design of the HORSE manufacturing control system architecture [HA16, Gre21].

3.2.8 The formal view revisited

An aspect framework defines a set of aspects for information system architectures. The set of aspects 'dissects' the overall architecture into aspect architectures. Each aspect architecture can again consist of a number of models. Recalling our formal definition of architecture from Section 2.4, we can insert the notion of aspect architecture into this definition.

Say we have a set A of aspects, containing k aspects denoted as a_i:

$$A = \{a_1, a_2, \ldots, a_k\}$$

Then the architecture $a(c)$ of a CIS c is a set of k aspect architectures, where we use the operator π as a projection operator onto a specific aspect:

$$a(c) = \{\pi_{a_1}(c), \pi_{a_2}(c), \ldots, \pi_{a_k}(c)\}$$

The division into aspects is one way of dividing an architecture into sub-architectures, as shown for the general case in Section 2.4. The aspect architectures do not typically form a strict partition of the overall architecture, as they may overlap in elements. If we take the UT5 framework, for example, databases are typically elements in the data aspect architecture (in which their internal data structures are further described) and in the system aspect architecture (in which their use by software components is described).

Each aspect architecture model can consist of sub-models (using the aggregation dimension explained in the sequel of this chapter). Each sub-model is again a model, which typically belongs into exactly one aspect architecture. This means that we can formulate the following design rule:

Each individual architecture model belongs to exactly one aspect of an explicitly chosen (and specified) aspect framework, unless there is an explicitly specified reason to combine aspects in one model.

The above rule can informally be paraphrased as 'stay in the box'.

This concludes our discussion of the aspect dimension of architectures. In the next section, we move on to the second dimension of architectures: the aggregation dimension.

3.3 Aggregation dimension

In the aggregation dimension, we determine how detailed an architecture model is with respect to the number of components identified in the model. The dimension ranges from very aggregated (few large components) to very detailed (many small components). We first discuss the principles of this dimension, then present examples for further clarification.

3.3.1 Principles

In typical architecture design efforts, we use architecture descriptions at several aggregation levels to describe things from a global, overall picture to a detailed picture. To do so in a top-down fashion, we explode (open up and refine) components at a higher level of aggregation into their components at a lower level of aggregation. This means that we traverse subsystem relations in the architecture structure. If we do this multiple times, we call this stepwise refinement. If we work in a bottom-up fashion, we do the inverse by combining (or collapsing) subsystems into their super-systems. If repeated, we call this stepwise aggregation.

The number of aggregation levels used depends heavily on the type of architecture under consideration. A quite elaborate example set of levels may be (as illustrated in Figure 22, with the highest level of aggregation at the top and the lowest level at the bottom):

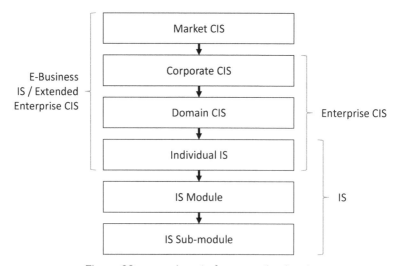

Figure 22: example set of aggregation levels

Market complex information system level: describes the architecture of the set of inter-organizational complex information systems supporting a market in which organizations exchange information; components are formed by corporate complex information systems.

Corporate complex information system level: describes a complete corporate complex information system (covering all information management in an entire organization) as one architecture model; domain complex information systems are components.

Domain complex information system level: describes a business information domain complex information system (covering information management within a specific business domain such as purchasing, finance, or human resource management) as one architecture model; individual information systems are components.

Individual information system level: describes an individual information system as one architecture model; main information system modules are components.

Information system module level: describes an individual information system main module as one architectural model; sub-modules are components.

Information system sub-module level: describes a sub-module as one architectural modules, where the functional elements in the sub-module are components.

It is good to note that where a specific set of aggregation levels is used (like the one in Figure 22), other terms may be in practical use that may be confusing. For example, the term *enterprise information system* (EIS) may coincide with several levels from the set of Figure 22: an EIS may cover the entire information system landscape of an organization (and hence be a corporate complex information system), it may cover one business domain (and hence be a domain information system), or it may cover multiple but not all domains (and hence be in between two levels). The latter situation can occur with the use of enterprise resource planning (ERP) systems. The term e-business information system or extended enterprise information system is even more complicated as it applies to multiple organizations (market level) but typically only covers a limited set of domains (domain level). So, it is always important to be explicitly clear about what is meant.

When we move from a specific aggregation level down one level (as shown by the arrows in Figure 22), we decompose (or explode) one or more of the components at the upper level. A component at the upper level corresponds to a number of components at the lower level, the functionality of which is usually a partitioning of the functionality at the higher level: all functionality is covered and there is no overlap. In other words, there are proper system-subsystem relationships between the levels.

Note that it is a design choice to decompose all components of a model into a single model at a lower aggregation level (as done in the example that follows), or to decompose each individual component into a separate model at the lower aggregation level. The first choice may be preferable when dealing with quite simple architectures, since it leads to an easy overview of the entire architecture. The second choice may be preferably when dealing with complex architectures with many components at lower aggregation levels. Here, stepwise refinement into multiple architecture models can be (and often should be) used to obtain separation of concerns with respect to the described functionality (leading to a proper modularization of the design).

3.3.2 Examples

In this section, we illustrate the principle of decomposition (refinement) along the aggregation dimension by means of three examples: a simple abstract example, a larger example of an airline business information system, and an elaborate example using the manufacturing process management system that we have introduced before in this chapter.

Abstract example

We first illustrate the concept of aggregation by a very simple, abstract example. For reasons of simplicity, we limit the example to the software aspect (see Figure 13). In Figure 23, we see a trivial architecture at the highest possible aggregation level: it shows only one single component (i.e., a *black box*). Clearly, this architecture is not very descriptive.

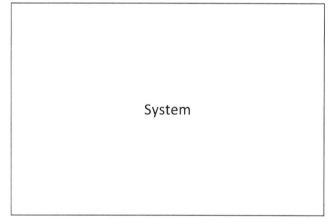

System

Figure 23: example abstract architecture aggregation level 1

When we decompose the trivial architecture, we arrive at the next aggregation level, as shown in Figure 24. We see two sub-systems, which together provide the same functionality as their super-system at Level 1.

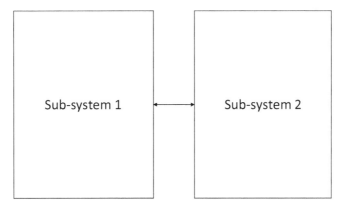

Figure 24: example abstract architecture aggregation level 2

In Figure 25, we see the same architecture at Aggregation Level 3. Sub-system 1 has been decomposed into three lower-level sub-systems (which we might call sub-sub-systems, but that becomes a bit confusing with more levels). These three sub-systems form a partitioning of Subsystem 1. The choice has been made not to further refine Sub-system 2. Note that all interface relations (arrows in the figure) of the part of the architecture that is decomposed must reappear consistently at the lower level. In other words: when going down the aggregation dimension, no information about the structure of the architecture should be lost.

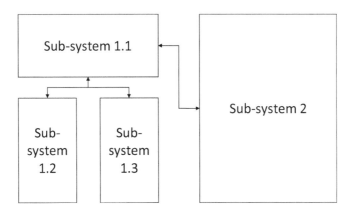

Figure 25: example abstract architecture aggregation level 3

Airline business information system example

In a more practical context, we can illustrate the principle of refinement with various aggregation levels of the architecture of the operations management information system (OMIS) of an airline company: Trans-Oceanic Airways (TOA). In Figure 26 to Figure 28, we show the top three aggregation levels for this architecture. We will return to the TOA architecture later in this book.

Figure 26 shows the black box view of the OMIS of TOA - this aggregation level is labeled as *Level 1*.

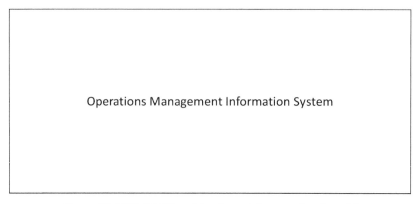

Figure 26: TOA OMIS architecture at Aggregation Level 1

The black box view of the TOA OMIS is decomposed (refined) into three business domain systems as shown in Figure 27, resulting in the software architecture at *Level 2*. This level coincides with the third level from the top in Figure 22: it shows how a corporate CIS is composed of business domain CISs. We have added a dotted box to indicate that all components are part of the same super-system one level up in the aggregation hierarchy. This makes it easier to understand the aggregation relations when analyzing the levels in a bottom-up fashion (from bottom to top in terms of Figure 22).

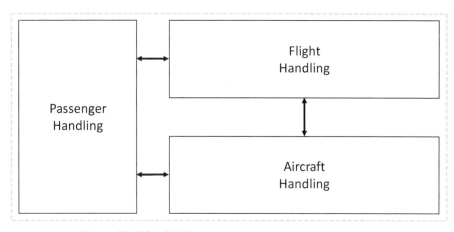

Figure 27: TOA OMIS architecture at Aggregation Level 2

Each of the three business domain systems can be further decomposed into individual business information systems. The result at *Level 3* is shown in Figure 28. This level coincides with the fourth level from the top in Figure 22: it shows how business domain CISs are composed of individual ISs[17].

---

[17] We explain the functionality of the individual ISs when we revisit this example in Chapter 7 of this book – in Section 7.3.1 to be precise.

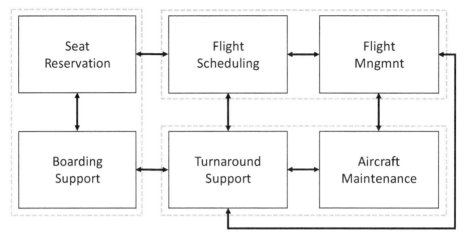

Figure 28: TOA OMIS architecture at Aggregation Level 3

Figure 28 shows how interfaces can also be refined when going down the aggregation dimension. Where there is one interface between *Flight Handling* and *Aircraft Handling* in Figure 27, there are three interfaces in Figure 28. These three interfaces together represent the same functionality (data flow) as the one interface at the higher level. If we add the data sets transferred between modules, the one interface at the higher level should cover all data sets of the three interfaces at the lower level.

Manufacturing process control system example

Our third example of stepwise refinement along the aggregation dimension is from the domain of manufacturing. Here we show how to refine the software architecture of a manufacturing process control system (MPCS), as we have already discussed in Section 3.2.5.

In Figure 29, we see the MPCS of Figure 16 in isolation. At *Aggregation Level 1*, the architecture is a black box without internal structure (analogously to Figure 23).

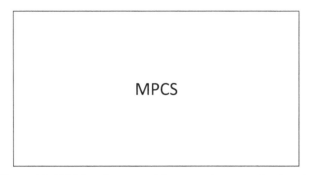

MPCS

Figure 29: MPCS software architecture at aggregation level 1

To refine the black box, we first determine that there is a *global level* of manufacturing control and *a local level*. The global level controls entire manufacturing processes across multiple manufacturing cells (workstations), for instance along a production line in a factory. The local level controls individual manufacturing cells. The result of refining the black box into these two levels is shown in Figure 30 at *Aggregation Level 2*. The two identified sub-systems both use data about the products that are manufactured. They obtain this data from the *product definitions* database.

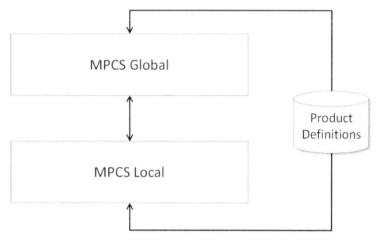

Figure 30: MCS software architecture at aggregation level 2

Note that typically, there will be one instance of the global level system and many instances of the local level system (as there may be many manufacturing cells) – we abstract from this aspect here for reasons of clarity.

To further refine the software architecture at *Level 2*, we determine that there is a design/configuration aspect to manufacturing control and an execution aspect. In the design/configuration aspect, the processes and their tasks and steps are designed and parameterized, as well as the agents that perform the steps (human workers and manufacturing robots). In the execution aspect, these processes and their elements are actually put to work by the agents. This leads to the software architecture at *Aggregation Level 3* as shown in Figure 31. We see that the two aspects are coupled by databases that contain the data of the manufacturing processes, tasks, steps and agents.

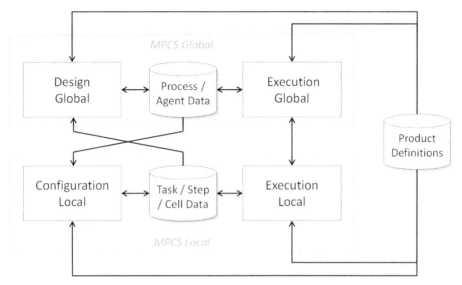

Figure 31: MCS software architecture at aggregation level 3

Note that at *Level 3* in Figure 31, we have exploded systems at *Level 2* into sub-systems and local databases at *Level 3*. We have also refined the interfaces between the identified subsystems. There is one interface between MPCS Global and MPCS Local at *Level 2* and there are three interfaces at *Level 3*. It is important to keep the relations between interfaces at aggregation levels consistent: the interfaces at a refined level should be parts of the interface at the aggregated level.

The four software systems at *Aggregation Level 3* can be further refined to *Aggregation Level 4* to further detail the functionality in these systems. The result is shown in Figure 32. For reasons of brevity, we omit the description of all modules in this architecture (for the readers interested: they can be found in [Gre21]).

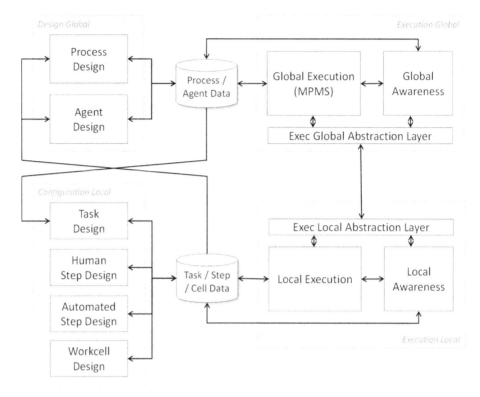

Figure 32: MCS software architecture at aggregation level 4

Even though the architecture shown in Figure 32 already has considerable complexity, the architecture in the project from which this example is constructed uses two additional levels of decomposition [HA16], leading to a much more detailed (and hence much more complicated) architecture. For reasons of brevity, we omit these two levels here.

3.3.3 The formal view revisited

In this section, we revisit our formal view of architectures, as started in Section 2.4.

When we move an architecture down the aggregation dimension, we decompose that architecture into sub-architectures. The first level of decomposition corresponds with the formal model we have discussed in Section 2.4:

$$a(c) = \{m_1(c), m_2(c), \ldots, m_n(c)\}$$

Each of the sub-architectures $m_i(c)$ can be further decomposed into a number (here shown as k) sub-sub-architectures to arrive at Aggregation Level 2:

$$m_i(c) = \{m_{i_1}(m_i(c)), m_{i_2}(m_i(c)), \ldots, m_{i_k}(m_i(c))\}$$

This decomposition process can be repeated if necessary (in the case of large, complex architectures), arriving at multi-level architectures (as illustrated in Figure 22).

The sub-architectures of an architecture (at each aggregation level) form a proper partitioning of the architecture: together, they cover the entire architecture and no components are replicated between sub-architectures.

3.4 Abstraction dimension

The next information system architecture dimension that we discuss is the abstraction dimension. We first describe the principles underlying this dimension and then present an example of the use of this dimension.

3.4.1 Principles

In the abstraction dimension of information system architecture, we determine how abstract or concrete an architecture description needs to be. In this dimension, completely abstract means that no concrete choices have been made with respect to components in the architecture (like functional software blocks in a software architecture). In other words, the elements of an architecture are described in very general terms. Conversely, completely concrete means that the components are described in very precise terms.

Going down the abstraction dimension means specializing the elements in an architecture. Here, specializing means sub-typing. Going up the abstraction dimension means abstracting the elements in an architecture, i.e., moving from a sub-type to its super-type.

There is no 'standard list' of values along the abstraction dimension, but we can illustrate it with an example. The abstraction dimension can consist of the following values:

1. Class type components: information system components are described in terms of general software system classes, indicating their functionality. An example is: data management system.

2. System type components: information system components are described in terms of general software system types. An example is: relational database management system (RDBMS) (which is a specialization of a data management system at the higher abstraction level).

3. Vendor type components: system components are described in terms of specific software system series from specific vendors. An example is: DB2 (which is an RDBMS of a specific vendor and hence a specialization of a general RDBMS).

4. Vendor version components: system components are described in terms of specific software systems from specific vendors including their versions. An example is DB2 Version 13 (which is a specific version of DB2 and hence a specialization of DB2).

Note that in the above example list, a higher number in the list actually means a lower level of abstraction. From this point of view, the dimension might be called the *concretization* dimension, but *abstraction* dimension is a much more common term.

Generally speaking, all components in a single architecture model should be of equal abstraction. A component that is more abstract than the rest may indicate that a decision has been postponed. A component that is more concrete than the rest may indicate that a decision has been taken too early. We can hence formulate the following general architecture design rule:

An individual architecture model is uniform with respect to the abstraction dimension unless there is an explicitly stated reason why this is not the case.

3.4.2 Examples

We illustrate the concept of abstraction by two examples: one in the software aspect and one in the data aspect (as in the UT5 model of Section 3.2.3). The latter shows that the abstraction dimension (and likewise the aggregation dimension that we have seen in the previous section) is not only applicable to the software aspect.

Simple example in the software aspect

Figure 33 shows a simple software architecture model that is *very* abstract as it only shows a structure but no indication of the functionality of the components. It specifies that there are four components of which the left hand three seem to have something in common (indicated by the numbering), and it specifies how the components are interconnected. Clearly, this is not very usable in practice (it would be at *Value 0* in the dimension values list discussed in Section 3.4.1).

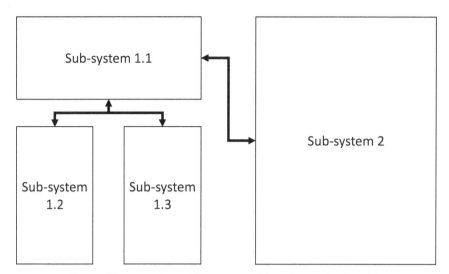

Figure 33: example architecture model at abstraction level 0

In Figure 34, we see a model of the same architecture but now specified at Abstraction Level 1. At this level, each component has an indication of the software system class it belongs to, hence making the description of the components more concrete than at *Level 0*. We see that the left-hand side of the architecture is the financial part and the right hand side the material handling part of a CIS. We also see that the financial part consists of a payment system and two interface systems.

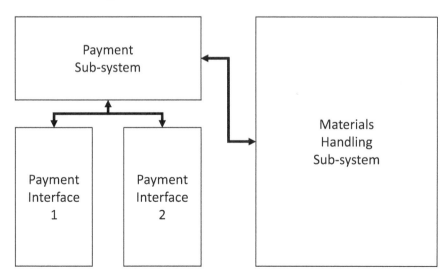

Figure 34: example architecture model abstraction level 1

Figure 35 shows a model of the same architecture again, but one more step down the abstraction dimension (we are now at Value 2). Here we see that each system class of the previous step is replaced by a software system type. The choice has been made for example that the Materials Handling Subsystem is an Enterprise Resource Planning (ERP) system.

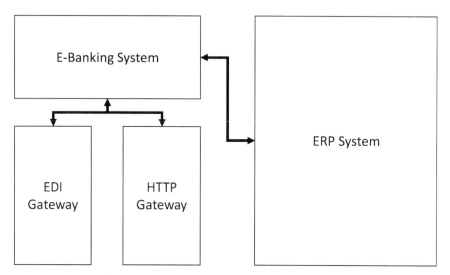

Figure 35: example architecture model at abstraction level 2

Figure 36 again shows the same architecture, but now at Abstraction Level 4 (for reasons of brevity, we have made two steps at once from the previous figure, so we have skipped Level 3): for each component, the vendor[18] and the version of the software is determined – this means that at this level of detail, no further concretization choices can be made (in the architecture design).

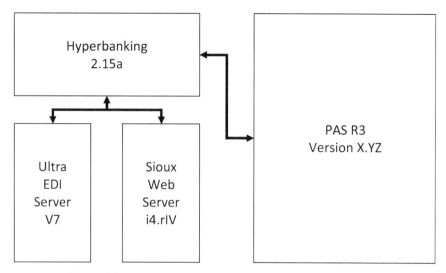

Figure 36: example architecture model at abstraction level 4

---

[18] Obviously, any similarity with names of existing software vendors is coincidental.

Example in the data aspect

To show an example of several abstraction dimensions in the data aspect, we can revisit the manufacturing domain example that we have seen before. In Figure 17, we see the data aspect architecture of the MPCS discussed there. In this data aspect, we find the element *event*. This is a fairly abstract element at *Abstraction Level 1*, which we can make more concrete along the abstraction dimension.

We can move to *Level 2* in the abstraction dimension by making things more concrete by subtyping. As shown in Figure 37, the *event* element can be made more concrete by showing that it can either be an *alert*, a *measurement*, or a *notification* (i.e., there are three sub-types). An *alert* is an event that represents an exceptional situation that requires handling (like a malfunctioning machine in a manufacturing cell). A *measurement* is an expected reporting of the value of something in the manufacturing process, like the temperature of a machine. A *notification* is an event that conveys some kind of status message, e.g., the notification of the completion of a production process.

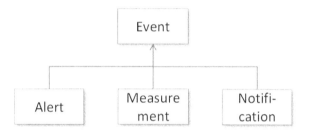

Figure 37: data aspect element at abstraction *level 2*

We can further make each of the three types more concrete down the abstraction dimension. In Figure 38, we show the concretization of the *alert* element at *Abstraction Level 3*. It shows that there three kinds of alerts, related to respectively activities (i.e., something has happened with a manufacturing process), agents (i.e., something has happened with an actor in a process), and general safety (i.e., some general safety threshold has been breached). We omit the concretizations of the other two elements of Figure 37 for reasons of brevity.

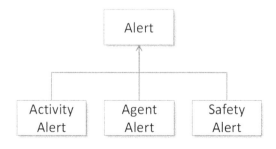

Figure 38: data aspect element at abstraction *level 3*

To show yet another level of concretization (i.e., one more level down the abstraction dimension), we can further specify the types of safety alerts at *Abstraction Level 4*. This is shown in Figure 39, which shows that safety alerts can be *global* (related to an entire production line of factory) or *local* (related to a single manufacturing cell).

Figure 39: data aspect element at abstraction *level 4*

3.4.3 Aggregation versus abstraction

We have now seen the aggregation and abstraction dimensions of information system architecture. These two dimensions are often confused in architectural practice, although they are very different dimensions. This confusion can lead to a bad understanding of the architecture under design and hence to poor designs.

Put very simply, one can state the difference between the dimensions as follows:

- moving in the aggregation dimension means changing the number of elements in an architecture description (decreasing when aggregating, increasing when refining), whereas the level of detail of the description (number of descriptive attributes) of each individual element remains the same;

- moving in the abstraction dimension means the opposite: the number of elements remains the same, but the level of detail of the description of each individual element changes: it decreases when abstracting (descriptive attributes are removed), it increases when concretizing (also called subtyping: descriptive attributes are added).

So, an architecture description can be very much aggregated, but still be very concrete – or very detailed and still very abstract. This observation is important in navigating through an architecture design space in an architecting project, as we discuss in more detail in Section 3.6.

3.5 Realization dimension

The *realization* dimension defines a number of levels ranging from architecture goals (i.e., *what* we want to accomplish with the systems described by an architecture) to means (i.e., *how* we want to accomplish things with an architecture).

The dimension can be interpreted as ranging from very business-oriented to very technology-oriented[19]. At the business end, we find specifications of the business elements describing the reasons for the existence of a CIS. At the IT end, we find specifications of technological structures enabling the realization of a CIS (i.e., the embodiment of a CIS architecture). As such, the realization dimension covers a broader range of specifications than pure CIS architectures (i.e., specifications of software systems only).

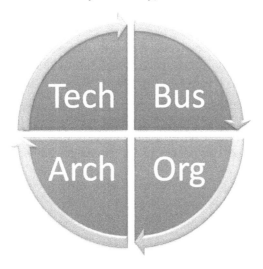

Figure 40: BOAT model [(taken from [Gre16])]

As an example operationalization of the realization dimension, we use the BOAT framework in this book. BOAT distinguishes four levels[20] [Gre16], typically shown in a circular fashion to depict their relationship in evolutionary development scenarios (see Figure 40):

---

[19] This is why this dimension was called 'Business-to-IT' dimension in older versions of this book.

[20] Note that these levels are called 'aspects' in the BOAT framework, as BOAT offers a cyclical alternative to a linear dimension [Gre16], as shown in Figure 40. As we do not consider the cyclical case and do not want to get confusion with the 'aspect' term as used in Section 3.2, we use the term 'level' in this book, as for the abstraction and aggregation dimension.

Business (B): the business level describes the business goals of an information system. As such it answers the question why a specific information system exists or should exist or what should be reached. Topics can be improvement of business process efficiency levels, support for new business functions, etcetera. How things are done is not of interest at this level.

Organization (O): the organization level describes how organizations are structured to achieve the goals defined at the B level. Organization structures and business processes are main ingredients here – automated systems are not yet in scope in this level. The O level is closely linked to the concept of enterprise architecture (see also Section 2.5).

Architecture (A): the architecture level covers the conceptual software structure (software architecture) of automated information systems required to make the organizations defined at the O level work. As such, it describes how automated systems support the involved organizations.

Technology (T): the technology level describes the technological realization of the systems of which the architecture is specified at the A level. The T level covers the concrete ingredients from information and communication technology, possibly including hardware, software, languages and protocols.

Of the above, the business level is sometimes hard to capture in structured graphical models (it cannot easily be formalized[21]) – it therefore often has a textual description (e.g., a list of requirements). Therefore, the business level does not really have the nature of an architecture model as discussed in Chapter 2 . The other three levels do have this nature: they contain architecture models (of organization, software, and technology) – even though in 'BOAT speak', only the A level has the 'architecture' label.

3.6 Combining dimensions into a design space

We have seen four architecture design dimensions in the previous sections of this chapter: the aspects, aggregation, abstraction and realization dimensions. In this section, we combine these dimensions into design spaces for architecture, i.e., conceptual spaces in which we can position architecture models and reason about design paths to and from them.

---

[21] In enterprise architecture approaches, we can find specification techniques for various kinds of *business goal models* though, like the OMG Business Motivation Model [OM15]. We do not cover these approaches in this book, as we focus on the architecture of business information systems – see the discussion in Section 2.5.

3.6.1 A four-dimensional design space

The four dimensions we have seen in the previous sections are in principle orthogonal. This means that we can choose the value in each dimension independently when designing an architecture model. This implies that the four dimensions actually create a four-dimensional design space in which we can position architecture specifications. This is illustrated in Figure 41 – obviously to the extent that four dimensions can be shown in a two-dimensional picture.

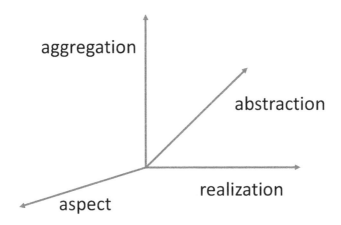

Figure 41: all four architecture dimensions combined

Each architecture model has a specific value with respect to the aggregation, abstraction and realization dimensions, and covers one or more specific aspects. In other words, each architecture model can be placed at a specific point in the design space of Figure 41. This positioning is comparable to geometry, where a point is placed in a three-dimensional space by means of its x-, y- and z-values.

Positioning an architecture specification in the design space is illustrated (or at least attempted to illustrate, again as 4-dimensional drawing is hard) in Figure 42. Here we see a specification positioned at the star symbol. It is positioned at *Level 4* in the aggregation dimension (so is rather detailed compared to the examples that we have seen so far), at *Level 3* in the abstraction dimension (so is rather concrete), at the *organization level* in the realization dimension, and in the *software aspect* in the aspect dimension. In trying to read the figure, you may see that the first three dimensions span up a 'regular' 3-dimensional space (as you may have seen in geometry), and we had to 'fiddle in' the fourth dimension from a graphical perspective.

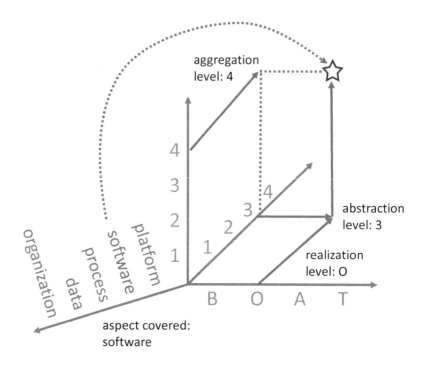

Figure 42: architecture specification positioned in four-dimensional design space

Two different architecture models can be at different positions in the design space, for example because one is more abstract than the other (and hence be at a different position with respect to the abstraction dimension). To get from one existing model to another existing model in an overall architecture specification, one has to navigate the design space, i.e., move along one or more of its dimensions.

To create a new model on the basis of an existing model in an overall architecture specification, one has to transform the model along the involved dimension(s). We have seen examples of this for the aggregation and abstraction dimensions in this chapter.

Obviously, it is not easy for the human mind to navigate a four-dimensional space (as illustrated by Figure 42). Therefore, we reduce the four-dimensional space to a three-dimensional space in the next subsection.

3.6.2 A three-dimensional design cube

When performing an architecture design process, we have to traverse the design space that we have seen in the previous subsection. In an architecting project, we often start with an abstract, highly aggregated, business-oriented architecture specification. In a number of design steps, we need to arrive at a concrete, detailed, IT-oriented specification (that is the basis for the realization of information systems). In doing so, we have to describe all relevant architecture aspects – the aspects in principle play a role at every abstraction, aggregation and realization level.

This means that we can transform the four-dimensional design space of Figure 41 into a three-dimensional space by keeping the abstraction, aggregation and realization dimensions explicit (the ones that we explicitly navigate), and making the aspect dimension implicit. Such a three-dimensional space is shown in Figure 43 in the form of what we call an *architecture cube*. This cube consists of cells (the small cubes in the figure). Each cell is identified by a combination of specific values in the aggregation, abstraction and realization dimensions. Each cell contains a set of architecture models: these models together describe the architecture at the specific levels of aggregation, abstraction and realization.

In Figure 43, we show an example design space with three abstraction levels (front to back), four aggregation levels (top to bottom) and four realization levels (left to right). The space is shown as a cube consisting of 3x4x4=48 cells, where each cell represents a specific combination of values along the three dimensions.

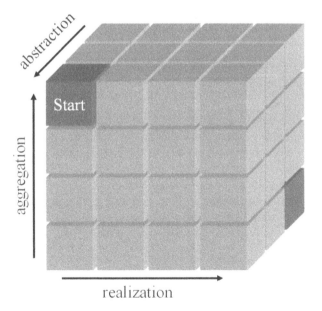

Figure 43: three dimensions combined

The architecture models in one cell of the cube deal with all relevant aspect dimension values for that cell. In other words: the aspect dimension is 'hidden' in the cells described by the other three dimensions ('implicit', as we have stated above) – this to keep the cube understandable to our thinking in at most three dimensions. This is illustrated in Figure 44, in which one cell (the top-right-front one) is opened to show that it can contain architecture models in various aspects following the UT5 model as discussed in Section 3.2.3.

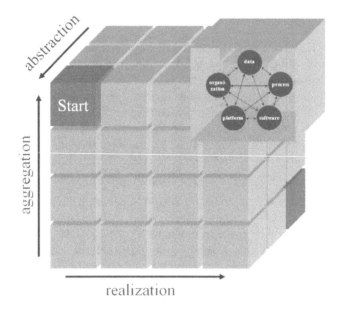

Figure 44: architecture cube with one cell opened

Performing a complete architecture design process now means going via a number of model transformations from the front top left cell (labeled 'Start') to the back bottom right cell (where the label 'End' is unfortunately invisible)[22].

Note that the values in each of the three dimensions are determined by the characteristics of the architecture design (or analysis) process at hand - and consequently so are the characteristics of the start and end cells of the cube. In a complete (C)IS architecture design process, the start cell contains a highly aggregated, highly abstract, non-realized (i.e., mostly in terms of requirements) specification of the architecture. The end cell contains a detailed, concrete, realized (i.e., in terms of specific software technology) specification of the architecture[23].

An individual model transformation in the cube means going from one cell to another cell. A sequence of transformations thus creates a modeling path. An example path from start to end in the design space of Figure 43 is shown in Figure 45. In this path, first two realization transformation steps are made, then

---

[22] This approach is an extension of the approach described in [Wie03], in which a two-dimensional design space is discussed.

[23] Typically, a detailed specification of the architecture of the hardware components on which the (C)IS will run is not included. In other words: a computer architecture is typically not included in a (C)IS architecture - and a VLSI architecture certainly not (see the discussion in Section 2.5.2).

three refinement steps along the aggregation dimension, next a third realization step, and finally two concretization steps along the abstraction dimension.

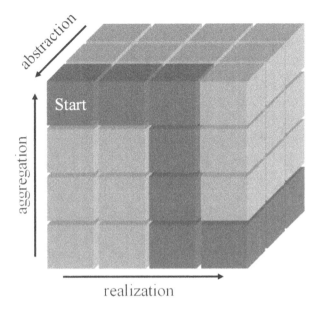

Figure 45: example path through the cube

Obviously, (many) other paths through the cube are possible too. Figure 46 shows an alternative path (note that part of the path is at the back of the cube and hence invisible in the figure). In this alternative path, most of the concretization along the abstraction dimension is performed earlier compared to the path in Figure 45 and most of the refinement along the aggregation dimension later.

The path of Figure 46 can be preferred over the path of Figure 45 if concrete choices have to be made between large components in a corporate information system architecture. An example is the design of the composition of a corporate information system from a small set of large COTS systems. In this case, the concrete systems can be chosen earlier in the architecture process, such that the refinement steps in the aggregation dimension can be made to fit the functionality of the chosen systems.

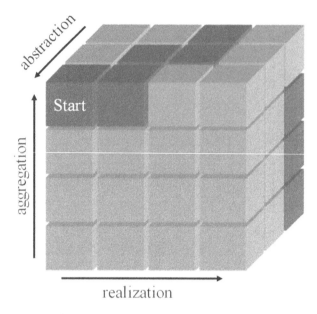

Figure 46: alternative example path through the cube

If two cells are adjacent in the cube (i.e., they touch sides), only one dimension needs to be reconsidered in a model transformation between the cells. Making only transformations between adjacent cells does require many transformations though to get from start to end in the cube – eight in the design space of Figure 43, as illustrated in Figure 45 and Figure 46. To reduce the number of transformations, we may move between cells that only touch with ribs or even only with corners – that reduces the number of transformation steps in the example to five respectively three. These transformations are more complex however, as they imply changes in two respectively three dimensions at the same time.

Note that an architecture re-engineering process (i.e., deducing the architecture from an existing, undocumented information system) implies traversing the cube in the other direction, i.e., from the end cell to the start cell. In this process, we start with a very concrete, detailed, IT-oriented description and have to move towards a specification that is more abstract, aggregated, and business-oriented.

3.6.3 An alternative three-dimensional cube

In the previous subsection, we have seen a three-dimensional architecture design cube that can be used to illustrate a design path through the aggregation, abstraction, and realization dimensions. This cube, however, leaves the aspect dimension implicit to avoid a four-dimensional 'cube' that would be very hard to understand.

Alternatively, we can make the aspect dimension explicit and make another dimension implicit. As an example, we have made the realization dimension implicit in the cube shown in Figure 47. For the aspect dimension, we have chosen the aspects of the UT5 framework as discussed in Section 3.2.3. Each aspect covers a vertical 'slice' of the cube, as illustrated for the software aspect.

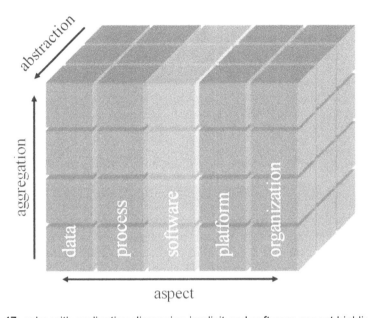

Figure 47: cube with realization dimension implicit and software aspect highlighted

The cube of Figure 47 can be used to explicitly address the relation between aspect models at various aggregation and abstraction levels, where the various realization steps are 'hidden' (implicit) inside the cells of the cube.

When we take out an aspect slice from the cube, we can indicate a per-aspect design path along the aggregation and abstraction dimensions. Figure 48 shows three alternative design paths (in blue) for the software aspect slice:

1. first refine along the aggregation dimension, then make concrete along the abstraction dimension;
2. first make concrete along the abstraction dimension, then refine along the aggregation dimension;
3. use a mixed approach, in which aggregation dimension and abstraction dimension are traversed in an interleaved way.

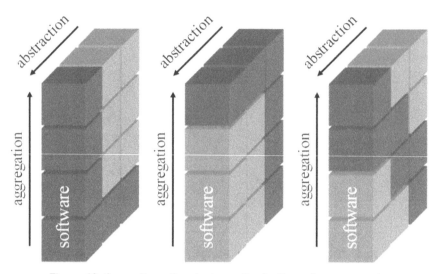

Figure 48: three alternative design paths for the software aspect

Note that each slice in Figure 48 covers the entire realization dimension (i.e., each cell contains models for all realization values). We can make the realization dimension for a single slice explicit by expanding the slice across the realization value (i.e., replicating the slice for each value in the realization dimensions). This results again in a three-dimensional cube as illustrated in Figure 49 for the software aspect. This cube is essentially the same cube as the one we started with in Figure 43, but now specialized for the software aspect only.

Obviously, we can do this aspect expansion for each individual aspect, which would bring us in the situation where we would have 'expanded' the cube that we started with in Figure 43 by replicating it for each aspect of the UT5 model. This means ending up with five three-dimensional cubes that together cover the four dimensions of the design space.

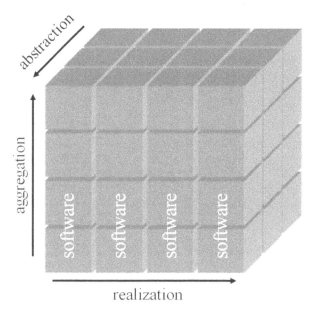

Figure 49: aspect slice expanded into a cube for the realization dimension

3.6.4 Traversing the design space in a structured way

How to structure a sequence of model transformations in a correct and feasible way is described by architecture frameworks and/or architecture design methods: these provide the 'cooking recipes' for the information system architect by specifying sequences of design process steps and (intermediate) results between these steps. In other words: they prescribe how to move through a design cube to obtain a good architecture design. This topic is further discussed in Chapter 5 of this book.

Apart from the prescriptions or suggestions in architecture design frameworks and methods, we can make some general observations:

- If an architecture under design describes a system of which the detailed functionality is very clear to start with, it is wise to first traverse the aggregation dimension to specify the functional structure of the architecture in detail. After that, the abstraction and realization dimension can be traversed.

- If an architecture design project is heavily technology-dependent (i.e., the system that is described by the architecture has to fit the structuring constraints of a specific information technology class), it is wise to give priority to traverse the realization dimension before proceeding too much in the aggregation and abstraction dimensions.

- If an architecture design project is heavily constrained by a pre-existing choice of preferred, concrete target systems (for example because these are part of a firm standard), it can be wise to give priority to traversing the abstraction dimension. We have seen this already in the design path of Figure 46 and its discussion.

4 UNDERSTANDING ARCHITECTURES IN STRUCTURES

The four architecture dimensions discussed in the previous chapter can be used to structure the architecture design space for business information systems. As such, they are a 'conceptual analysis toolbox' to deal with the complexity of architectural design. But the question is now how to fill the 'coordinates' in this design space, i.e., how do we actually design new architecture models? Do we have a 'conceptual synthesis toolbox' for that too that helps us deal with the complexity? In answering these questions, we focus on the product-oriented face of architecture (see Section 2.2) in this chapter – the process-oriented face follows in the next chapter.

In the building world, new architectures are typically designed on the basis of well-established structures – proven knowledge is reused to make the design process more efficient and its outcomes more predictable. In the IS architecture world, comparable structures have been and are being developed that also allow for reuse of existing structures. In this chapter, we discuss these structures for IS architecture design.

We can distinguish between three classes of structures, each of which is treated in this chapter. We begin with architectural styles that define general, high-level design approaches that influence overall architecture structures. Next, we pay attention to architectural patterns, which specify substructures in architectures that have a repeating character across different architectures[24]. The third class that we discuss contains reference architectures, which are abstract blueprints

---

[24] Note that the terms *style* and *pattern* are not uniformly used by all authors in the domain. For example, sometimes the term *style* is used for what we call *pattern* [Zhu05].

for (parts of) IS architectures. We treat the three classes one-by-one for didactic reasons but elements from the three classes can be used in parallel in practical architecture design efforts.

4.1 Architecture styles

Architectural styles are well-known in the building domain. They were already in common use millennia ago: see for example Figure 50, which shows fragments from buildings conforming to three main architectural styles in the classic Greek history. Each style represents another approach to building: the Doric style is basic and concentrates on simple construction; the Ionic style is more ornamental and adds aesthetics to the design; the Corinthian style is very elaborate and aims at showing the wealth (and hence power) of the owner of a building. A bit less long ago, we find for example the Roman, Gothic and Baroque styles for designing churches, with a more or less similar development.

Figure 50: Doric, Ionic and Corinthian column styles (sources unknown)

In this section, we apply the concept of architecture styles in the domain of information system architectures. Architecture styles determine the overall structure of architectures as conceptual designs, but also influence the choice of technologies chosen for the realization of systems following these architectures (as we discuss in Chapter 8 on architecture embodiment). To some extent, architecture styles for information systems engineering can be compared to programming paradigms for software engineering[25].

Below, we first discuss the concept of architecture style. Then, we present a simple catalogue of styles. We discuss the interesting styles from the catalogue

---

[25] As an example [Mar18], three paradigms for software engineering can be distinguished: structured programming, object-oriented programming, and functional programming.

in a bit more detail. As architecture design may benefit from the characteristics of multiple styles, we pay attention to the combination of styles. We end this section with revisiting the formal view on architectures, applied to the concept of architecture style.

4.1.1 The concept of architecture style

We can define the concept of architecture style as follows:

> *An architecture style is a generally recognized structure class describing the overall structure of an architecture at a high level of abstraction (and indirectly the process of architecting).*

As the definition states, an architecture style primarily defines how the main structure of architectures appears, and thereby the artifacts that are realized on the basis of this architecture. Revisiting the analogy of the Greek architecture styles, we see that the Doric style leads to simple and functional buildings, the Ionic style leads to more ornamental buildings, and the Corinthian style to buildings that are meant to impress.

Architecture styles are also used in information system architectures. Here, the emphasis is clearly not on ornamental or aesthetic aspects (see the discussion in Section 2.5), but on structural aspects: an architecture style defines characteristics of the overall structure of architecture models. In other words: styles constrain the structure of architecture models. Put more formal: an architecture style is a set of constraints on the structure of allowed architecture models. Like with the buildings, a choice of an architecture style determines the characteristics of the information systems realized along the architecture design.

Although architecture styles can in principle be applied to all architecture aspects (see Section 3.2), they are most commonly used to structure the software aspect (referring to the aspect framework shown in Figure 13). We therefore start with discussing styles for the software aspect below. Further on in this section, we briefly discuss styles for other architecture aspects.

4.1.2 A simple software aspect style catalogue

There is no generally accepted catalogue of architecture styles for the software aspect. We can form a simple catalogue, however, by distinguishing four very basic styles (shown in Figure 51):

Monolithic: the monolithic style uses a black-box approach: all functionality is included in one monolith and hence there is a complete absence of explicit structure.

Layered: the layered style defines structure by organizing functionality into several layers of functional abstraction, i.e., each layer (except the bottom one) builds on the one below it.

Columned: the columned style defines structure by organizing functionality into several functional 'sub-areas' (the columns) at the same level of functional abstraction, i.e., the columns are complementary in functionality.

Component-Oriented: the component-oriented style defines structure by grouping coherent application functionality into components with explicit interfaces to allow them to exchange information and hence collaborate, without the necessity to explicitly order these components.

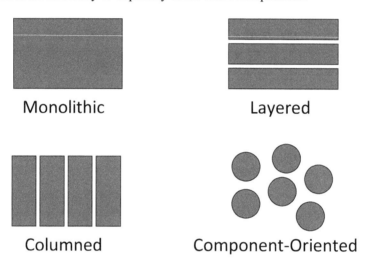

Figure 51: basic IS architecture styles

We discuss the three structured styles in more detail in the three subsections below.

4.1.3 Layered style

The layered architecture style defines the structure of an architecture by distinguishing several layers of functional abstraction[26] that are stacked. We illustrate this in Figure 52. In principle, there can be an arbitrary number of layers. The minimum number obviously is two (otherwise the layered architecture 'degenerates' into a monolithic architecture). In practice, we find layered architectures with varying numbers of layers. The popular three- and four-tier architectures have (as their names suggest) three respectively four

---

[26] Note that functional abstraction is different from architectural abstraction as introduced in Section 3.2.8: functional abstraction abstracts in terms of an application domain (related to 'what' an information system should do) whereas architectural abstraction abstracts from characteristic of modules of the information system (related to 'how' the information system should be realized).

layers (we discuss these in Chapter 6 in the section on multi-tier architectures). The ISO-OSI networking architecture contains seven layers [Wi24m].

In the layered structure, every layer but the lowest one makes use of the functionality of the underlying layer to realize its own functionality. This use takes place via well-defined interfaces that abstract the functionality of the underlying layer. A layered style is also referred to as a stratified style, where a stratum is a layer.

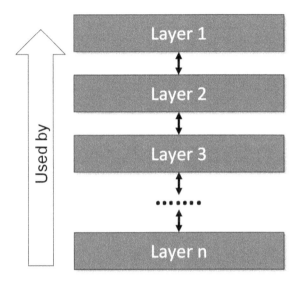

Figure 52: structure of an architecture with a layered style

To understand the principle of layering, we can use an analogy with the building domain, where one part of a building is based on an underlying layer (in this domain, the term 'based' is interpreted in a very physical sense). Figure 53 shows an example, in which we see two layers or strata, in which the lower one forms the 'basement' of the higher one.

Figure 53: layering in building architecture: the levels of the Louvre in Paris, realized in different building periods (photo by author)

In the information system domain, a layered architecture style supports *vertical modularity* of architectures, where *vertical* refers to the principle of functional abstraction. This form of modularity allows evolution of an architecture on a per-layer basis (where a layer is a module in this style), if interfaces between the layers are well-defined.

In a strictly layered style (i.e., the pure use of the style), a layer makes use of only the layer directly below it. In a loosely layered style, a layer can make use of all layers below it, i.e., bypass layers.

An example architecture following the layered style is shown in Figure 54. Here we see an architecture with four layers. As each layer only uses the layer below, it is a strictly layered architecture. The architecture describes the information systems of an insurance firm. In the lowest layer, we find the back-office systems, which are used to administrate the basic products of the firm (like individual insurance products). In the second layer from the top, we find the front-office systems which are used to manipulate composed insurance products at the client level. Between these two layers, we find the mid-office system layer, which contains the systems that make the connections between clients and basic products. Finally, the top layer contains the Web interface systems that are used to give employees of the firm and clients access to the front-end systems through the Internet. The downward arrows in the figure represent the requests of abstracted functionality of the underlying layer. The upward arrows represent the results returned to the requesting layer. For example, the Web Interface

Systems layer may request data to fill a web form from the Front-Office Systems layer and receive these data. The Web Interface Systems layer does not have to be aware how this data is created: the underlying functionality is abstracted.

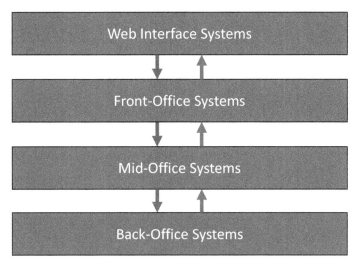

Figure 54: example architecture with layered style

An important application of the layered style is in the distinction between applications and infrastructure – we discuss this in Chapter 6 .

4.1.4 Columned style

The columned style defines structure by distinguishing several functional 'sub-areas' (which form the columns), i.e., it uses the principle of separation of concerns with respect to functionality within one functional abstraction level. The columned style is illustrated in Figure 55. There can be an arbitrary number of columns – well, at least two since otherwise the style degenerates to a monolithic style. An important difference with the layered style is that the columns do not have a functional order. Even though they have a graphical order in an architecture diagram (like in Figure 55), this has no strict functional meaning. Consequently, each column can use the functionality of each other column (as illustrated by the arrows in the top and bottom of the figure).

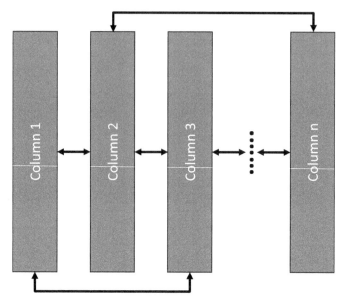

Figure 55: columned style

We can again use an analogy with the building domain to explain the columned style: in the building domain, we can distinguish several functional areas in a building that have specific functions and therefore different concerns for their design. A house may for example have a living area, a sleeping area, and a garage area, between which doors are the interfaces (as shown stylized in Figure 56). Even though in a diagram the areas are drawn in an order, they do not have a functional order: the garage area is not before or after the sleeping area.

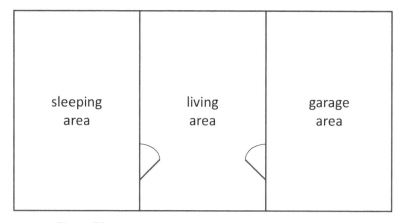

Figure 56: columned style in an abstract house floor plan

In the information systems domain, a columned architecture style supports *horizontal modularity* in architecture design. This form of modularity allows evolution of an architecture on a per-column basis (where a column is a module in this style), if interfaces between the columns are well-defined.

An important application of the columned style is the distinction between various basic business functions – we discuss this in detail in Section 6.2. A simple example is shown in Figure 57. Here we see (part of) the architecture of an insurance firm in a columned style, where each column contains the systems that support a specific business function.

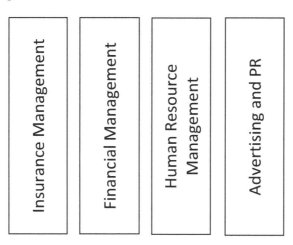

Figure 57: example architecture with columned style

The lack of strict ordering between columns can be observed in the example of Figure 57, where systems in the Financial Management column communicate with systems in all other columns (about billing customers, paying employees, and paying advertisers respectively). As a consequence of the lack of order, we have not drawn any connections between the columns in the figure, as this may result in creating a fully connected graph.

Sometimes, the columns are not so obvious in an architecture, but identifying them can help in analyzing the groups of stakeholders for the systems designed in an architecture project. Take the simple system architecture of Figure 15. In the way it is shown, no columns are visible. But if we reorganize the diagram, we get the architecture of Figure 58. As shown in the figure, now we see three columns. Each of these columns has its system end user stakeholders: salespeople for the External Relations column, externally-oriented bookkeepers for the External Finance column, and internally-oriented bookkeepers for the Internal Finance column.

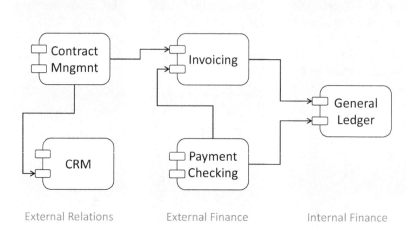

Figure 58: columned version of the architecture of Figure 15

4.1.5 Component-oriented style

The component-oriented architecture style defines structure by grouping coherent application functionality into components and encapsulating this functionality from its environment by the definition of explicit interfaces of the components. In terms of conceptual basis, it can be compared to the object-oriented paradigm in the software engineering domain (following the comparison that we hinted at in the introduction to the overall section). Components can communicate with each other freely: there are no rules like in the layered style. Components are not necessarily at the same level of functional abstraction, like in the columned style. The component-oriented style is illustrated in Figure 59, where we see a simple topology of six components.

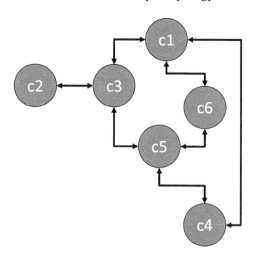

Figure 59: illustration of the component-oriented style

As there are no strict rules for the topology of the component-oriented style (which leads to a rather 'arbitrary' diagram to illustrate it, like Figure 59), it is up to the architect who uses the style to bring a logical ordering into an architecture following this style. Often, this is done by combining the component-oriented style with another style. We discuss this topic in Section 4.1.6.

Important (and well-known) sub-styles of the component-oriented style are:

Object-oriented architecture: in this style, architectural components are treated as objects, following the object-oriented programming paradigm, but at the aggregation level of information systems instead of program code. An object contains application functionality. The functionality is offered to its context through *methods*, which are specified in the object *interface* (or *signature*). Objects collaborate in an object-oriented environment that typically supports tight coupling of functionality (we discuss more technical details in Chapter 9 where we discuss infrastructures for coupling).

Service-oriented architecture: in this style, components are services, which contain application functionality like in the object-oriented style. Unlike the object-oriented style, the service-oriented style assumes an environment with loose coupling between objects, usually with dynamic service discovery. The technical context is often Internet-based (also here, we discuss technical details in Chapter 9 on infrastructures for coupling). The service-oriented style is applied in *service-oriented architecture* (SOA).

Microservice architecture: this is a variation on the service-oriented architecture with components that are services [New21]. In this variation, emphasis is on proper design of the interfaces between the components to keep the communication structure as simple as possible. These interfaces are typically called APIs (application programming interfaces). For this reason, this style is sometimes referred to as *API-based architecture*.

As an illustration of the component-oriented architecture style, a (very simple) example of an abstract service-oriented architecture of a distributed materials buying/selling system in the healthcare domain is shown in Figure 60. Here, we see an architecture consisting of 9 information system components, located across two organizations: Organization A is the buyer, Organization B is the seller. The components are connected (as shown by the arrows in the figure) to be able to collaborate and fulfill the business goal of the system.

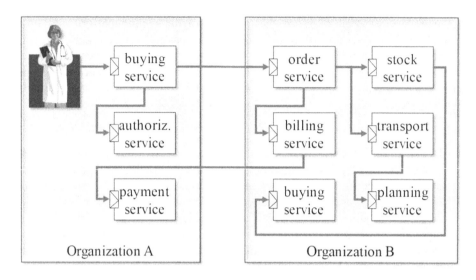

Figure 60: simple example architecture with service-oriented style

4.1.6 Combining styles

In modeling complex architectures, the use of a single architectural style can be too restrictive. For example, only using a layered style does not provide guidance for organizing things inside a layer. The same goes for the columned style, where things inside columns need to be organized. Only using a component-oriented style can lead to a lack of overall organization (in the end resulting even in a 'spaghetti-like' architecture structure). In these situations, a combination of styles can be used to model complex architectures.

To combine styles, one style is usually embedded into another style. This means that one style provides the overall structure, and another style is used for the structure 'inside' the elements of the overall structure.

A typical example is the combination of the component-oriented style and the layered style, as illustrated in an abstract fashion in Figure 61. Here, the component-oriented style is embedded in the layered style to organize the components into layers. The result is a stratified component-oriented architecture. Note that the interfaces between objects follow the strict layering principle: objects communicate only with other objects in the same or an adjacent layer.

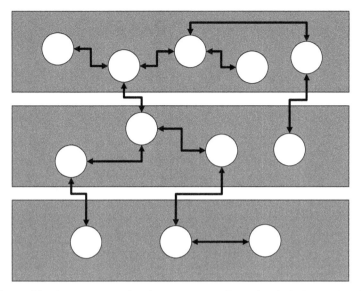

Figure 61: abstract example of component-oriented style in layered style

Obviously, we can make similar combinations of the component-oriented style and the columned style, or of the layered and columned styles.

In the case of complex architectures, the combined styles can be applied at different aggregation levels to manage the complexity. As an example, the architecture in Figure 61 can be modeled at two aggregation levels (and hence a set of several architecture diagrams): a higher aggregation level modeling the three layers as black boxes, and a lower aggregation level with three architecture models that each describe the components in a single layer. This reduces the complexity of each diagram, but possibly at the loss of the overview of component-to-component connections between the layers (this needs then to be described by more detailed specifications of the interfaces between the layers).

4.1.7 Styles in an application example

To illustrate the use of styles in analyzing an example application architecture, we show a simple architecture in Figure 62. Here, we see the software aspect architecture of a travel agency, consisting of 12 software modules (application systems) and 5 databases. The software modules can be seen as components, making this an architecture with a component-oriented style. The emphasis in this style is on modularization of functionality without further organization of the modules (i.e., the components).

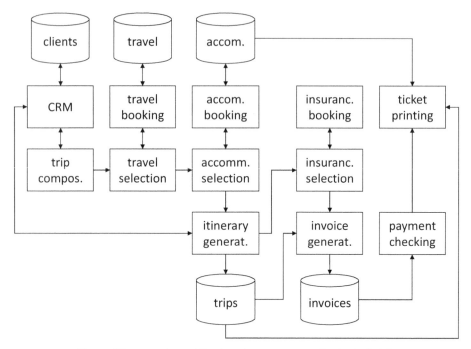

Figure 62: example architecture in a component-oriented style

We can, however, also decide that it is important to distinguish between front-office support and back-office support in the architecture. This yields the architecture of Figure 63, which has a layered style (with an embedded component-oriented style as discussed in the previous subsection). We can aggregate the modules in each of the indicated layers into a single module at a higher aggregation level (as discussed in Section 3.3), yielding a basic layered model with two layers.

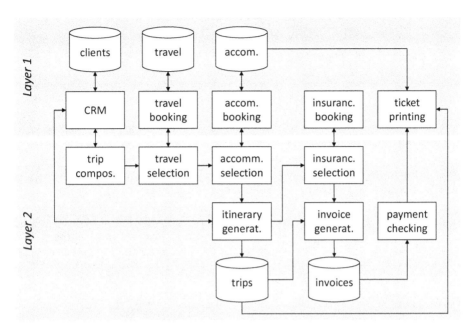

Figure 63: example architecture in a layered style

Starting from the architecture in Figure 62, we can also decide that the modules should be organized per business function in the travel agency. This results in the architecture of Figure 64, which has a columned style with five columns (with an embedded component-oriented architecture, as discussed in Section 4.1.6). As discussed in Section 4.1.4, there is a 'free' communication topology between the columns, visible in interfaces that cross multiple columns in the diagram.

If we wish, we can aggregate the modules per indicated column in Figure 64 to a higher aggregation level, resulting in a basic columned architecture with five black-box columns.

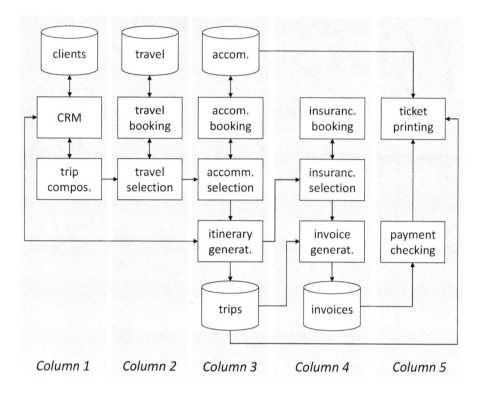

Figure 64: example architecture in a columned style

This example shows that the use of a specific architecture style is a design choice, made on the basis of the intended purpose and of the design strategy of the architecture. If the design strategy is to construct the architecture from a general basis, the layered style is appropriate. If the design strategy is to construct the architecture in an incremental fashion per business function, the columned architecture is appropriate.

4.1.8 Styles for other architecture aspects

So far, we have focused on the software aspect in this section on architecture styles. But styles are also applicable to other architecture aspects as we have seen them in Section 3.2.3 on the UT5 framework.

The four architecture styles that have been discussed for the software aspect (see Figure 51) are based on very abstract principles like separation of abstraction levels (layered style) or separation of functional concerns (columned style). Hence, they can also be applied to the other four architecture aspects (see Figure 13). For reasons of brevity, we do not go into all possible combinations but illustrate this observation with one aspect.

As an example, we can consider the data aspect and apply the four identified architecture styles to this aspect:

- In a monolithic data architecture, all data is considered to be in one universal set (abstract database).

- In a layered data architecture, data is distributed over various abstraction levels, e.g., for various business decision levels (operational, tactic, strategic).

- In a columned data architecture, data is distributed according to various information system functions, e.g., related to system functions. We see an example of this in Figure 64, where we have databases per business function (even though the relation here is not strictly one-on-one).

- In a component-oriented data architecture, subsets of data can be placed within components (this is well-reflected in the object-oriented sub-style, in which data can be encapsulated within objects).

Apart from the above, one may distinguish aspect-specific styles. For example, one can argue that the data organization paradigms (such as relational, functional, network and object-oriented paradigms[27]) are data aspect styles.

4.1.9 The formal view revisited

Architecture styles constrain the structure of architecture models: they describe what models should be structured like. Put in other words: an architecture style is a set of constraints on the set of allowed architecture models.

Formally, we can express this latter interpretation as follows, where S is a style in the form of a set of constraints s_i, and AS is the set of architectures a conforming to this style (expressed by the predicate *conforms*):

$$S = \{s_1, s_2, \dots, s_n\}$$
$$AS = \{a \mid (\forall s_i \in S)(\text{conforms}(a, s_i))\}$$

4.2 Architecture patterns

As we have seen before in this chapter, architecture styles define 'overall' structures for architecture models. But in composing these models, we often need to make 'local' design decisions that influence structures within these models, not the models as a whole. Architecture *patterns* can be used here to reuse general structures that have proven to be helpful in the design of good architectures. The use of architecture patterns is intended to have a positive impact on quality attributes of architectures, such as maintainability, portability and implementability [Har07].

---

[27] We revisit these data organization paradigms when we get to data management technology in Section 8.2.1.

To use a well-understood analogy, we can look again at the building domain. Here, architectural patterns may for example define ways to organize rooms in a building with respect to each other (illustrated in Figure 65): rooms may be connected in a walk-through sequence (a linear pattern, practical for a museum) or they may all be connected to a central hall (a star-shaped pattern, practical for an office building). The patterns do not relate to the overall organization of a building (like an architectural style), but rather a local organization of architectural elements within a building.

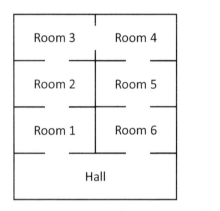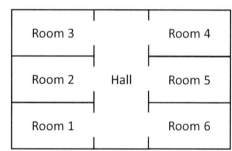

Figure 65: two patterns for connecting rooms in a building:
linear (left) and star-shaped (right)

Below, we first discuss the concept of pattern in information system architectures. Next, we focus on patterns for the software aspect of information system architectures. We then continue with a discussion of patterns for other architecture aspects.

4.2.1 The concept of architecture pattern

The concept of architecture pattern can be defined as follows:

> *An architecture pattern is a generally recognized recurring (sub)structure that is used to describe part of the overall structure of an architecture.*

Patterns can be seen as abstract building blocks providing parts of the structure of architecture models. In other words: a pattern is a part of an architecture model that can be reused (like a modeling 'macro')[28]. Patterns can be composed to form more complex structures, for example complete architecture models. Composing of patterns can be performed by linking patterns to each other or by embedding one pattern into another pattern.

---

[28] In the building world, patterns are used in architecture design, sometimes referred to as 'organizations' [Chi96]. These patterns place architectural elements in space, to form for example centralized, linear, radial, clustered or grid organizations of elements.

In architecture design, patterns are guidelines for creating good structure. As such, they are indeed elements in a 'conceptual construction toolbox' as mentioned at the start of this chapter. In other words, architectural patterns improve partitioning the functionality of systems and promote reuse of design knowledge by providing solutions to frequently recurring problems [Rah17].

In architecture analysis, patterns are usable tools as well: they can be used as guidelines for identifying well-established structures within an architecture design, i.e., structures that have proven their usefulness and that can be easily communicated.

4.2.2 Patterns for the software aspect

Even though patterns can be used for all architecture aspects of the UT5 framework, patterns are most commonly used for the software (application logic) aspect of information system architectures. In other words: they are used as conceptual tools to design the structure of the software of the information system under design.

A pattern toolbox usually has the form of a pattern catalog. In the catalog, patterns are listed (often with a graphical illustration) with their relevant attributes like:

- name: the identification of the pattern;

- description: an explanation of the purpose of the pattern;

- application: the description of the places where the pattern may be usable;

- requirements: the requirements the pattern has on its environment to be indeed usable.

There are several 'bibles' available that describe general software pattern catalogs[29], like [Bus96, Fow96, Sch00, Rah17], as well as pattern catalogs for specific aspects of software design, like [Zim23]. Here, we discuss two pattern catalogs for illustrative purposes. We start with a very simple catalog below. After that, we discuss a more complex, multi-level catalog.

---

[29] Note that there is an overlap of the field of patterns for software design (in software engineering) and the field of patterns for information system design: they share many design principles, be it at a separate level of aggregation (and abstraction) – as we have seen in Section 2.5.2. There are patterns for software design, however, that are not so relevant for information system design because they address problems that typically appear at the software engineering level. An example is the model-view-controller (MVC) pattern [Tay10, Rah17] that is used to design user interfaces and their control.

4.2.3 A simple pattern catalog for the software aspects

In Figure 66, we see a graphical version (omitting the textual specifications) of a very basic pattern catalog for the software aspect. This catalog identifies four patterns to connect architecture components (i.e., it is an integration pattern catalog): *direct invocation, file transfer, shared database* and *shared bus*.

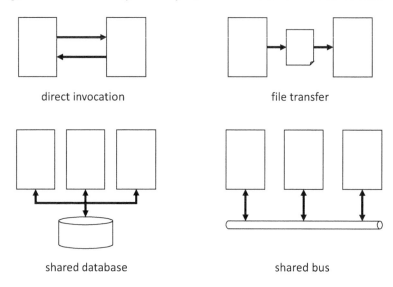

direct invocation   file transfer

shared database   shared bus

Figure 66: very basic pattern catalog in graphical form

The interconnection concepts (*file, database* and *bus*) in the catalog are used at the conceptual level here: they are not (yet) related to any technical implementation. Implementation (also called *embodiment*) is discussed in Chapters 8 and 9 of this book. In embodiment, an abstract interconnection concept is often related to a 'similar' concrete interconnection concept (technology), but not always necessarily so (as an existing technology context may dictate a specific embodiment design decision).

The four patterns are further described in Table 1, providing the specification attributes introduced above. In each row, we see the name of a pattern, a short description highlighting its nature, an indication for what purpose it can be applied, and the requirements that must be met to allow application of the pattern in an architecture. So, we may consider Table 1 the actual pattern catalog and Figure 66 a graphical aid to illustrate the patterns in the catalog.

Table 1: basic interoperability pattern catalog in tabular form

Name	Description	Application	Requirements
Direct Invocation	remote procedure invocation between modules	(synchronous) one-to-one module coupling	modules must be active simultaneously
File Transfer	file transfer between modules	offline (batch-wise, asynchronous) 1-to-n module coupling	existence of predefined file structure
Shared Database	data transfer via shared database	flexible asynchronous n-to-m module coupling	existence of predefined shared database, availability of transaction management
Shared Bus	data transfer via bus	direct (synchronous) flexible m-to-n module coupling	existence of standardized bus, modules must be active simultaneously

4.2.4 A hierarchical pattern catalog for the software aspect

In Figure 67, we see a graphical representation of a pattern catalog for the software aspect (based on [Bas03]) that contains more patterns than the very simple catalog of Figure 66. To provide an overview of the patterns, they are organized into a taxonomy, i.e., a hierarchical classification. The taxonomy allows finding a right pattern for a design problem by making a series of choices.

The taxonomy of Figure 67 starts with the abstract *Pattern* class of patterns. This root class is subtyped into five main classes of patterns (the children of the root class at the second level of the taxonomy). Each of these five classes has children again (at the third level of the taxonomy). Most of these children are patterns (not pattern classes). An exception is the class *Event Systems*, which again has children. This taxonomy thus contains 12 patterns, organized by means of 6 patterns classes (not counting the root class). For clarity, the pattern classes are colored gray, the patterns are colored white in the figure. Obviously, a pattern catalog like the one in Figure 67 can also be described in a table like Table 1 – we discuss this a bit later.

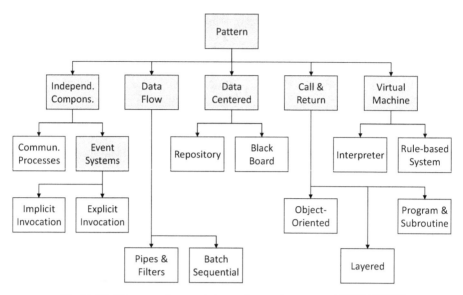

Figure 67: bigger pattern catalogue for system aspect [based on [Bas03]]

We briefly discuss the contents of the taxonomy by going through the five main pattern classes at the second level of the taxonomy:

Independent Components: This pattern class describes software structures consisting of elements that each have been designed as independent modules that collaborate in one of two modes. The first mode is message passing (the Communicating Processes pattern) in which explicit, content-based messages are exchanged between modules. The second mode is based on exchanging events (the Event Systems class), in which modules collaborate by reacting on events generated by other modules, which can be passed either implicitly or explicitly.

Data Flow: This pattern class describes software structures where the modules are arranged in a sequence, such that the data output of one module in the sequence is the data input of the next module in the sequence. The data can be passed either in a continuous way (the Pipes & Filters pattern), such that all modules are active at the same time. The data can also be collected at the beginning of the data flow and next be processed in a batch-wise way (the Batch Sequential pattern), such that the modules are active one-by-one.

Data Centered: In the Data Centered pattern class, we find patterns in which the collaboration between software modules is based on the principle that these modules share a common storage for data, in which they can store data and from which they can retrieve data. In the Repository pattern, this storage contains structured elements (like in a database). In the Black Board pattern, the storage is unstructured (such that it can contain arbitrary data elements).

Call & Return: In this pattern class, modules collaborate by directly invoking each other's functionality: they call each other and expect a specific return. As such, the modules are coupled more tightly than in the three classes above. The Program & Subroutine pattern is a traditional software pattern with typically very tight coupling. The Layered pattern follows the principle of functional abstraction. The Object-Oriented pattern is based on method invocation between objects. This latter pattern is often used with object-oriented middleware, which we discuss in Section 9.6.

Virtual Machine: In the Virtual Machine pattern class, one module executes a task specification that is provided by another module. In the context of business information system architectures, this task specification is of a high-level, business-oriented kind. Examples are a business process specification which is interpreted by a business process management engine (the Interpreter pattern) or a set of business rules interpreted by a business rule engine (the Rule-Based System pattern).

Note that the Call & Return patterns class contains a Layered pattern. This pattern is in its objectives similar to the layered architecture style that we have discussed in Section 4.1.3. In our use of the concepts of style and pattern, however, we apply a layered style at the level of an entire architecture, whereas a layered pattern is used in a local structure within an architecture.

The patterns in the taxonomy can be described in a tabular catalog like the one shown in Table 1, but to keep the structure, we need multiple levels. We show a partial catalog (partial for reasons of brevity) in Table 2 for the Data Flow and Data Centered pattern classes of Figure 67.

Table 2: Part of system aspect hierarchic pattern catalog

Data Flow Class			
Name	**Description**	**Application**	**Requirements**
Pipes & Filters	sequential array (with output-input coupling) of concurrently operating modules	stepwise processing of data elements in a streaming fashion	modules must be active simultaneously
Batch Sequential	sequential array (with output-input coupling) of sequentially operating modules	stepwise processing of data elements in a batch-wise fashion	modules must support batch-wise output and input interfaces
Data Centered Class			
Name	**Description**	**Application**	**Requirements**
Repository	set of modules interacting asynchronously through a shared, structured data repository	collaborative, asynchronous processing based on a shared, structured set of structured data	existence of predefined structured shared database, availability of full transaction management
Black Board	set of modules interacting asynchronously through a shared, unstructured data repository	collaborative, asynchronous processing based on a shared, unstructured set of unstructured data	existence of predefined shared database, availability of loose transaction management

4.2.5 Relating pattern catalogs

We have seen two pattern catalogs in the previous subsections: a small catalog with basic interoperability patterns for the software aspect and a more elaborate catalog with more general software aspect patterns. We can relate these two catalogs when we see that basic interoperability patterns can be used for the description of the interfaces between modules in more general software aspect patterns. Such a relation between pattern catalogs can be described by a table like the one shown in Table 3. In this table, we see an indication which interoperability patterns are typically used for the communication in the more general patterns.

Table 3: relation between pattern catalogs

Patterns	Direct Invocation	File Transfer	Shared Database	Shared Bus
Commun. Procs.	X			X
Implic. Invoc.				X
Explic. Invoc.	X			X
Pipes & Filters	X			X
Batch Sequential		X		
Repository			X	
Black Board			X	
Object-Oriented	X			X
Layered	X			X
Program & Subr.	X			
Interpreter	n.a.			
Rule-based Syst.	n.a.			

Note that the interoperability patterns do not apply to the patterns in the Virtual Machine class (Interpreter and Rule Based System), as in this software aspect pattern class, there is only one component involved - it either interprets a high-level program (for instance in a domain-specific language [Fow10]) or executes a specification specified as a set of rules (for instance a set of business rules).

4.2.6 Patterns in an application example

We can apply the pattern catalog of Figure 67 to the travel agency application architecture that we have introduced in Section 4.1.7. We do not try to be complete here in analyzing the application architecture but give two examples of patterns in this architecture - leaving the identification of other patterns to the reader.

When we look at the business functions supported by the modules in the architecture, we can see that there is a sequence of use of the modules in the processing of client orders: trips are composed, travel means are selected, accommodation is selected, an itinerary is generated for the client, insurance is selected and an invoice is generated (as indicated by the grayed software components and bold arrows in the figure). This sequence indicates a data flow pattern class (where the data flow is 'driven' by a customer order), as illustrated in Figure 68. If we assume that each individual customer order is processed when it arrives (i.e., orders are not batched for processing), we have a Pipe & Filter pattern as listed in the catalog of Figure 67. Note that we have not included the payment checking and ticket printing components in the pattern for two reasons. Firstly, these components may rely on batch processing: their functionality can be activated by a time trigger (like once daily or twice weekly) rather than by a customer order. This means that the involved data flow has different characteristics. Secondly, they are coupled to the identified data flow via a database, which typically indicates temporal decoupling (i.e., not the continuous flow typically associated with a data flow pattern).

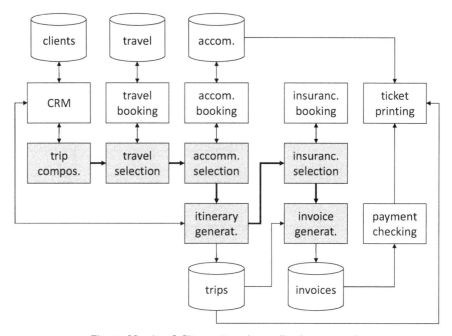

Figure 68: pipe & filter pattern in application example

Patterns in the Data Centered pattern class can typically be easily identified around databases in a software aspect architecture: this pattern occurs if multiple software modules communicate via a database. An example in the travel agency architecture is illustrated in Figure 69, where we see how generated invoices are stored in a database for later use in payment checking. If we assume that this is a structured database (which makes sense for an administrative scenario), we can identify the Repository pattern (again indicated by the grayed software components and bold arrows in the figure).

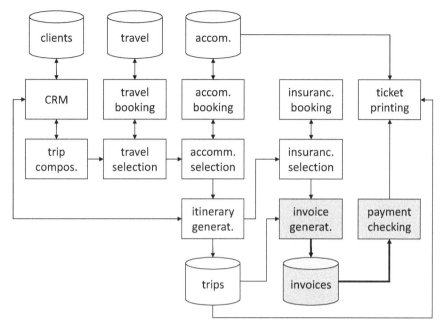

Figure 69: repository pattern in application example

4.2.7 Patterns for other aspects

As indicated before, patterns are mostly used for the software aspect of information system architectures. They are applicable to other aspects too, however, such as the data and process aspects. To illustrate this with an example, we describe a well-known pattern in the data aspect below. For the process aspects, a catalogue of business process patterns can be found in [Aal03].

The *star data model* is a data aspect pattern that is commonly used for data warehousing applications[30] [Kel97]. As informally illustrated in Figure 70, the pattern consists of a *facts* class surrounded by a number of *data dimension* classes. The *facts* class contains records of the basic facts kept in a data warehouse. The *data dimension* classes contain records of the descriptive dimensions of facts.

---

[30] We take a look at the software aspect of data warehousing applications in Chapter 7 of this book.

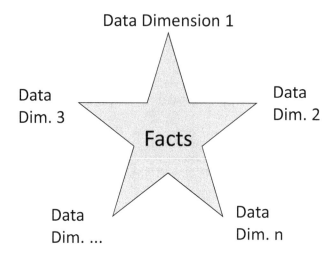

Figure 70: star data pattern principle (based on [Kell97])

In Figure 71, we see an example application of the star data pattern from the retail domain. Here, the central facts class contains sales records for individual sales. The four classes surrounding it contain the records that describe the sales: the time of a sales transaction, the product that was sold, the staff member who made the sale, and the store at which the sales transaction took place.

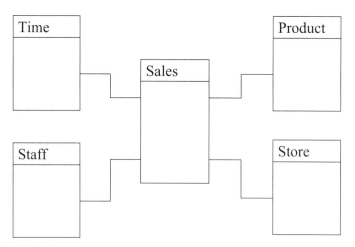

Figure 71: star data pattern example for retail (based on [Kell97])

4.3 Reference architectures

Styles and patterns as discussed in the previous section provide architecture structures in an application-independent way: they are not linked to specific functions of information systems. For recurring application types in the information systems domain, it is however helpful to have high-level, general architecture designs that can be reused and tailored for specific situations, like general blueprints – such that the wheel does not need to be reinvented over and over again. These architecture designs are called *reference architectures*. Reference architectures are getting increasingly important given the fact that the complexity, scope and size of systems is quickly increasing and the dynamics of their development as well as demands on integration are quickly increasing as well [Clo09].

Reference architectures are heavily used in other design domains. A good example is the building domain, where many abstract blueprints exist for classes of houses that are reused many times. In the Netherlands, for example, we commonly see the reference architecture *semi-detached house with slanted roof*[31], which is generally accepted as a standard for typical middle-class housing (shown in Figure 72, where the block contains two houses). Houses that comply with the reference architecture have strong structural similarities in their structure, but differ in the ways details are filled in.

Figure 72: example of semi-detached houses with slanted roof (source unknown)

Below, we first discuss the concept of reference architecture in the information system domain. Next, we show a few example reference architectures. Then, we compare the concept of reference architecture to that of *standard architecture*.

---

[31] In Dutch, this type of house is called 'twee-onder-één-kap', which translates into 'two-under-one-roof'. Everybody in the Netherlands with any interest in housing immediately recognizes this concept, showing the communicative power of reference architectures.

4.3.1 The concept of reference architecture

We can (loosely) define a reference architecture for the information system domain as follows[32]:

> *A reference architecture is a general design (abstract blueprint) of a structure for a specific class of information systems, using a chosen set of architectural aspects.*

Reference architectures in the (business) information system domain often focus on the software aspect of information system architectures, i.e., they are software system models. They may include elements of other aspects as well, however, or even focus on other aspects[33]. Reference architectures that focus on other aspects than the software aspect are often called *reference models*. An example is a business process reference model [Fet06].

The scope of a reference architecture is typically an information system or a combination of information systems. A combination of information systems can be intra-organizational (in the context of a corporate information system) or inter-organizational (i.e., a networked e-business system [Gre16]).

A reference architecture can in general be *descriptive* or *prescriptive*. A descriptive reference architecture describes a standard in a specific context based on the existing state of the art of that context. An example is a reference architecture that is built from best practice cases. A descriptive reference architecture can be used in analysis of concrete architectures or as inspiration for the design of new architectures. A prescriptive reference architecture describes a standard that is obligatory to follow to fit into a specific context. An example is a reference architecture that is the basis for interoperability in an e-business setting, where the reference architecture prescribes the structure of e-business systems to allow them to cooperate.

A reference architecture is often approved (or preferably even certified) by an organization that has the authority to do so, for example a standardization organization or a governmental body. We do, however, also see reference architectures defined by research or commercial organizations without 'official' approval or certification.

A reference architecture is elaborated for a specific situation to obtain a concrete architecture for a specific information system (or a standard architecture, as we

---

[32] There has been discussion on what precisely a reference architecture is (see for example [Clo09]), but for this book we take a pragmatic approach.

[33] In the context of governmental information system developments, we may find reference architecture documents that are to a large extent composed of guidelines on the development of information systems. As such, these documents concentrate on the organization aspect. If these guidelines are not linked closely to structures in other aspects (predominantly the software aspect), one might ask whether these documents contains reference architectures, or are building guides.

will see in the sequel). Elaboration can take place in various ways (which can be combined):

- A reference architecture can be elaborated by further detailing it along the aggregation dimension (see Section 3.3).

- A reference architecture can be parameterized, i.e., made more concrete along the abstraction dimension (see Section 3.3).

- A reference architecture can be extended by adding additional components to it, i.e., its scope can be extended.

The 'contents' of a reference architecture are based on knowledge of the domain for which it is designed – preferably on a generally accepted reference model for that domain. The main part of the contents is usually a description of an information system structure. This structure is often based on one or more architecture styles and a number of architecture patterns (and sometimes one or more other, more abstract reference architectures). This leads to the design process shown in Figure 73. Note that styles and patterns can be used also when applying (detailing, extending) the reference architecture – as shown by the dotted arrow in the figure.

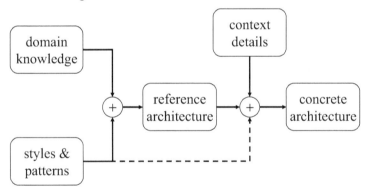

Figure 73: reference architecture process

Next to a structural description of an information system, a reference architecture can (or even should) contain:

- A specification of the authority that approved or certified it, plus a description of its governance process (stating who can change it in which ways).

- An explicit specification of the domain knowledge, styles and patterns used in the design of the reference architecture (see Figure 73).

- A set of guidelines of how to use the structural description in designing a concrete architecture.

- A set of criteria to check whether a concrete architecture conforms to the reference architecture.

101

Many reference architectures exist for (parts of) information systems. Some reference architectures are independent of specific (business) application domains and address system functionality that recurs across domains; some are specific for an application domain. An example of the latter in the transport domain is the Connected Vehicle Reference Implementation Architecture [Ite15]. A classification of reference architectures is provided in [Ang12]. This classification links classes of reference architectures to their intended use.

In the three subsections below, we present a few examples of reference architectures for individual systems (hence at the IS level), of reference architectures for enterprise integration (hence at the enterprise CIS level), and of reference architectures at the inter-organizational level (hence at the extended enterprise CIS or e-business IS level – see also Figure 22).

4.3.2   Reference architectures for individual systems

Reference architectures for individual systems describe the structure of a single information system. These systems can be general purpose or dedicated to a specific abstracted business function. One of the earliest reference architectures for general-purpose systems is the ANSI/SPARC reference architecture for database management systems [Tsi78]. More contemporary examples for dedicated systems are the ERA reference architecture for e-contracting systems [Ang08] and the Industrial Internet Reference Architecture (IIRA) [Lin17].

To further illustrate the concept of reference architecture for individual systems, we discuss two reference architectures for workflow management systems (or business process management systems) below: one developed by a standardization body, and one developed in academic research. The reference architectures describe the same class of concrete systems but are set up from different perspectives.

WfMC reference architecture

Figure 74 shows the reference architecture for a workflow management system as defined by the Workflow Management Coalition (WfMC – see www.wfmc.org) [Hol95]. This reference architecture is in fact a high-level system aspect model, outlining the main components of a workflow management system and the interfaces between these components. We discuss this architecture in more detail in Chapter 7 where we discuss architectures of concrete systems.

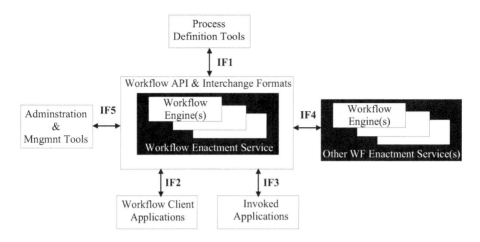

Figure 74: WfMC reference architecture for WFMS (from [Hol95])

Mercurius reference architecture

An alternative reference architecture for workflow management systems is that developed in the Mercurius research project [Gre98]. The top-level model of this reference architecture is shown in Figure 75. This too is a system aspect model, but it includes an explicit link to the data aspect architecture (it shows how data stores are connected to the system components). This reference architecture also provides an elaboration along the aggregation dimension (see Section 3.3): it elaborates the internal structure of the main components of the top-level model. As an example, Figure 76 shows an elaboration (explosion) of the WF Server component of Figure 75. A third refinement level (one further step down the aggregation dimension) is described too in the reference architecture specification [Gre98] - we discuss this further in Section 7.2.1.

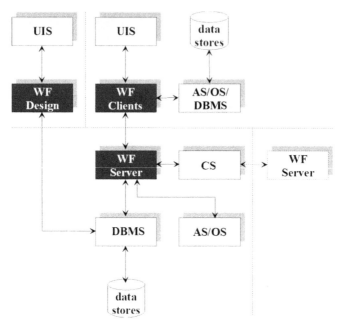

Figure 75: Mercurius reference architecture for WFMS, aggregation level 1

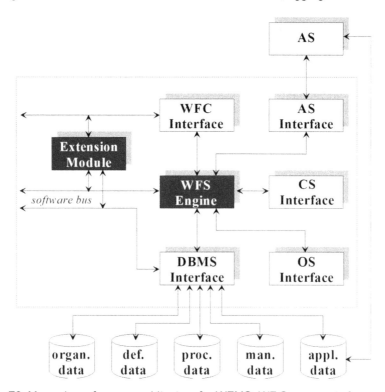

Figure 76: Mercurius reference architecture for WFMS, WF Server part of aggregation level 2

More reference architectures have been developed for the area of business process management, like BPMS-RA [Pou19], but we do not discuss them here for reasons of brevity.

4.3.3 Reference architectures for enterprise integration

In the previous subsection, we have discussed reference architectures for individual systems. In this subsection, we move our attention to reference architectures that are used to connect multiple individual systems, i.e., reference architectures for enterprise integration. This kind of reference architectures does not focus on the decomposition of specific functionality (such as that of a workflow management system), but focuses on interoperability issues between systems that provide specific functionality. Hence, these reference architectures often describe structures related to the use of middleware, i.e., software technology designed for accommodating interoperability. We address the technical aspects of middleware in more detail in Chapter 9 of this book.

To illustrate the concept of reference architecture for enterprise integration, we again provide two example reference architectures: one based on the object-oriented software paradigm from the end of the 20th century, and one based on the more recent service-oriented software paradigm. The former is not in broad attention anymore but provides a nice example of a well-structured reference architecture.

Object Management Architecture

A well-known reference architecture for object-oriented enterprise integration reference is the Object Management Architecture (OMA) defined by the Object Management Group (OMG) [OMG04]. The basic version of OMA is shown in Figure 77.

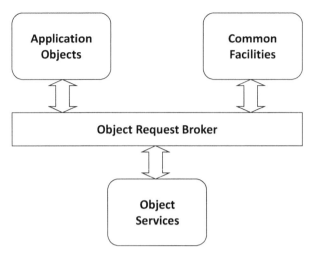

Figure 77: basic Object Management Architecture

The OMA reference architecture describes that in a complex, object-oriented software environment, software modules (objects) are to be divided into three main classes. The Object Services class provides modules with low-level, general functionality. The Common Facilities class provides modules with high-level, general functionality. The Application Objects class contains the modules with application-specific functionality. All modules interact using a software infrastructure called the Object Request Broker (ORB). This part of OMA has a reference architecture by itself, called the Common Object Request Broker Architecture (CORBA). We discuss more details of OMA and CORBA in Chapter 9 on middleware technologies.

SOA Reference Architecture

A well-known service-oriented reference architecture for enterprise integration is the SOA Reference Architecture by The Open Group [TOG09] – where SOA is an acronym for Service-Oriented Architecture. An overview of this reference architecture is shown in Figure 78.

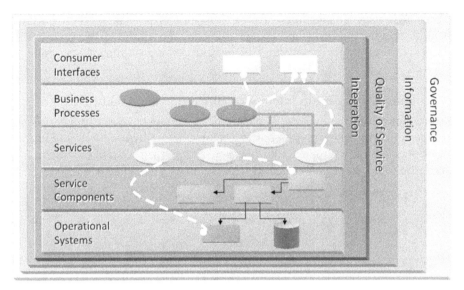

Figure 78: The Open Group SOA Reference Architecture overview (taken from [TOG09])

Where the OMA reference architecture focuses on the system aspect (is mainly concerned with software structure), the TOG/SOA reference architecture has a broader scope, taking for example also governance into account.

Another prototype reference architecture for the application of service-oriented technology but designed for the paradigm of service-dominant business, can be found in [Gre13]. This reference architecture is designed for application in the context of the BASE/X business engineering framework [Gre15].

4.3.4 Reference architectures for inter-organizational integration

Information systems of multiple autonomous organizations become more and more connected to support networked e-business [Gre16]. To allow this connection, these systems should be interoperable, i.e., be able use each other's functionality and exchange data among each other. One important way to enhance interoperability is to have the involved systems comply with a reference architecture that focuses on the connection between the systems, i.e., a reference architecture at the inter-organizational level.

Some reference architectures in this class address specific aspects of business ecosystems. A good example is the Reference Architecture Model of the International Data Spaces Association [IDS19], which addresses the data management aspect in business ecosystems. There is a gray area here between reference architectures for business collaboration (which aim mainly at the functional level) and reference architectures for middleware (which aim mainly at the technical level) – we address the latter in Chapter 9 of this book.

Often, reference architectures at the inter-organizational level are geared towards specific business application domains. To illustrate this, we briefly discuss two examples below in the domains of e-government and mobility services.

E-Government: European Interoperability Reference Architecture

An example from the domain of electronic government (e-government) is the European Interoperability Reference Architecture (EIRA) [PW15]. EIRA is meant to increase interoperability between European government systems. As an illustration, Figure 79 shows the high-level overview of EIRA.

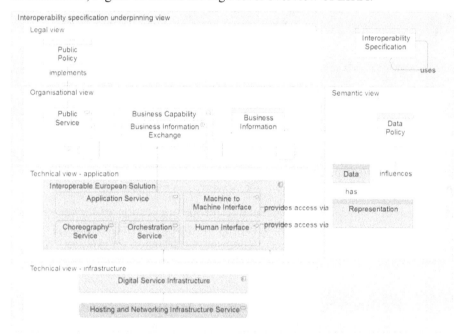

Figure 79: High-level overview of EIRA ^(taken from [PW15])

The EIRA overview is organized in five domains, which are in four *views*[34]. The *technical view* defines the structure of the general-purpose infrastructure for business services and the structure of the application systems (we discuss this distinction in general terms in Chapter 6). The *organizational view* defines the structure of services and information offered by the technical view. The *semantic view* defines the structure for managing the meaning of data in the technical and organizational views. Finally, the *legal view* describes the structure for the policies that govern the use and exchange of data.

---

[34] Note that these views have some relation to the views (or aspects) that we discuss in Section 3.2, but can certainly not be mapped one-to-one to these.

Note that the EIRA architecture may appear to have a layered architecture style (as discussed in Section 4.1.3), but the elements in the right-hand side of Figure 79 do not fit in a strict layering. Consequently, the style of this reference architecture has to be classified as component-oriented (as discussed in Section 4.1.5).

Mobility Services: Dutch Reference Architecture

To support interoperability between parties providing elements in cooperative mobility services (for example traffic management), a reference architecture has been developed by a consortium of partners in the Netherlands [Sam15]. The technical view of this architecture is shown in Figure 80. Note that this architecture is of a more technical nature than most of the architectures discussed in this book.

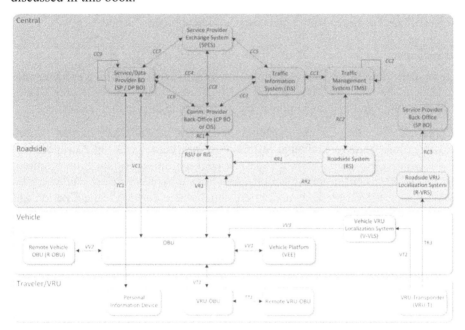

Figure 80: Technical view of Dutch C-ITS reference architecture (taken from [Sam15])

The structure of the reference architecture is clearly based on a layering in the application domain it is intended for: the highest level covers centralized mobility-related systems (such as central traffic management systems); the second level covers local systems placed along roads; the third level covers local systems embedded in vehicles (such as in-car systems); the lowest level covers systems related to individual road users (travelers or so-called 'vulnerable road users', who may carry for example smartphones with mobility-related apps).

At a first glance, the reference architecture appears to have a clear layered architecture style with four layers. Closer inspection, however, reveals that there are connections between components that 'cross' layers (for example the connection VC1 that crosses one layer and connection TC1 that even crosses two layers in the figure) – hence, it is a loosely layered architecture (see Section 4.1.3). If we aggregate the bottom three layers into one single layer, the architecture does have a strictly layered style with two layers (corresponding to the central components respectively the decentral components).

4.3.5 Reference architectures for other architecture aspects

The reference architectures that we have discussed so far are mainly focused on the software aspect of the UT5 aspect framework (see Section 3.2.3), i.e., for specifying reusable software structures. Reference architectures can in principle be used, however, for all of the UT5 aspects. To illustrate this, we discuss reference architectures for the data aspect and the process aspect below.

Data aspect

In the data aspect of business information system architecture, we use reference data architectures for the specification of reusable data structures. These reference data architectures are also called reference data models (RDMs).

Reference data models are especially important in industry domains where organizations heavily exchange information in a digital way, like in electronic commerce. Here, the reference data model is the basis for the 'common language' between the organizations. Organizations involved in promoting the use of such reference data models are the Centres for Trade Facilitation and Electronic Business (CEFACT) that exist within the United Nations (UN) and the Economic Commission for Europe (ECE). An example of a high-level promotion is a white paper explaining the overall use of an RDM [CEF17]. An example of an operational guideline is the one for supply chain management support [CEF16]. An example data architecture diagram from this guideline is shown in Figure 81. This diagram shows an example master data exchange structure, which is the basis for the definition of digital documents exchanged between parties in supply chains.

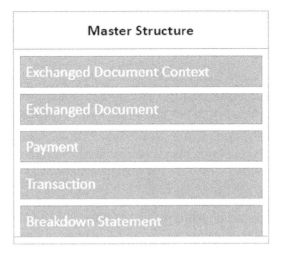

Figure 81: example Master Data Exchange Structure (taken from [CEF16])

Process aspect

In the process aspect of business information system architecture, we use reference process architectures for the specification of sets of abstract process models that form the basis for the realization of concrete sets of business process models, also referred to as business process architectures [Dij16]. Reference process architectures are also referred to as business process frameworks.

An example of a business process framework is the Cross Industry Process Classification Framework (PCF) of APQC [APQ24], which contains a very detailed classification (taxonomy) of standard business process activities. The activities in the PCF are organized in five aggregation levels (in the aggregation dimension as we have discussed in Section 3.3):

1. Category: a set of business processes related to main organizational functions such as supply chain management, finance and human resource management.
2. Process Group: a group of coherent processes within a category.
3. Process: an individual process that has a concrete business goal, like customer invoicing; a process consists of activities.
4. Activity: a key step in the execution of a process; an activity consists of tasks.
5. Task: an element of work that is part of an activity.

4.3.6 Reference architectures versus standard architectures

A reference architecture provides an established, 'ideal' abstract structure for an information system or set of information systems. A reference architecture is often designed in a top-down fashion with well-structuredness as main goal – this to facilitate other quality attributes when using the reference architecture in the design of concrete architectures. The design of a reference architecture may be based on other, more abstract, reference architectures. In the design of a reference architecture, stakeholder types may be involved, but no concrete stakeholders are distinguished in the design process (i.e., the reference architecture is not designed to suit one or more specific parties, such as specific business organizations).

A *standard architecture*[35] describes a standardized structure for a specific set of architectures (e.g. sites of a distributed organization) in the context of a specific organization. As such, its design is governed by a single user organization. A standard architecture may be designed in a bottom-up fashion, abstracting from a set of existing concrete architectures. But ideally, a standard architecture is related to one or more reference architectures. A broad acceptance by a concrete set of stakeholders within an organizational context is a main goal in the design of a standard architecture.

Standard architectures are instantiated to concrete architectures in the specific organization context they were designed for. These concrete architectures are typically related to specific IS (re)design projects and can hence be called project architectures.

The relation between reference, standard and concrete architectures is shown in Figure 82. The vertical dimension in this picture coincides with the abstraction dimension discussed in Section 3.3.

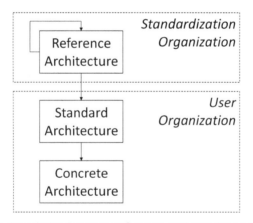

Figure 82: the relation between reference and standard architectures

In the design of standard architectures, reference architectures should ideally be used as a basis for two main reasons. Firstly, reference architectures are based

---

[35] Note that the term 'standard architecture' is not standard – other authors may use different terms like 'organization-specific reference architecture'.

on established knowledge, thereby providing means to enhance the quality of standard architectures. Secondly, using a reference architecture as a basis enhances the possibilities of interoperability of systems based on the standard architecture with systems in the world around the organization, as they may be based on the same reference architecture.

Where a standard architecture is abstracted enough to be 'lifted' from a concrete organizational context, it can become a reference architecture. Preferably, this process involves the participation of a standardization organization to ensure proper quality and acceptance of the resulting reference architecture.

5 ARCHITECTING WITH RECIPES

In the previous chapters, we have seen ingredients for understanding and structuring information system architectures. These ingredients are conceptual tools for the architecting process, but do not describe the architecting process itself. To paraphrase this in terms of cooking dinner: the ingredients for the dishes are there, but the cooking recipes are still missing. These recipes are the topic of this chapter. In other words: in this chapter we focus on the process-oriented face of architecture as discussed in Section 2.2.

The process-oriented face of architecture contains several classes of ingredients, each of which have a different goal and use. We discuss the following five classes - each in a separate section in this chapter:

- We start this chapter in Section 5.1 with the discussion of *architecture design frameworks*, which provide contexts for architecture design methods.

- Next, we turn to *architecture specification techniques* in Section 5.2. These techniques are based on languages in which we can express architectures - and often instructions how to use these languages.

- Then, in Section 5.3, we pay attention to *architecture design approaches*, i.e., overall approaches to structure architecture design processes.

- Fourth, we discuss *architecture design methods*, which are the actual 'complete' recipes for the architecture design process. This is covered in Section 5.4.

- Finally, we discuss *architecture principles* in Section 5.5, which are guidelines for architecture design processes that can be used to complement the above four classes.

Architecture design methods are often explicitly based on (or linked to) elements from the former three classes: they use frameworks, specification techniques and design approaches as elements in the description of the method. Architecture principles often have a 'looser' relation to the other classes. These relations are illustrated in Figure 83.

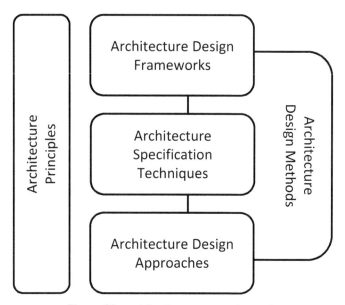

Figure 83: architecting process elements

Note that in practice, the four classes are not so precisely delineated: products 'marketed' in a specific class may contain elements from other classes. For example, if an architecture specification technique contains elaborate instructions how to use the technique in a well-structured fashion, it contains architecture design method elements.

Products in each of the classes can be supported by software tools that help applying these products. For example, an architecture specification technique can be supported by a graphical architecture editing tool based on that technique. An architecture design method can be supported by a project management tool that is based on the method to keep track of completed activities and plan future activities prescribed by the method.

5.1 Architecture design frameworks

An architecture design framework provides a general thinking context in which a concrete architecture design process can be placed. A discussion of characteristics of and differences between architectural frameworks can be found in [Gre06][36].

We discuss two example architecture design frameworks in this section: the Zachman framework and the MDA framework. These two frameworks are artifact-centric: they focus on models (the artifacts) to be developed with the aim to structure these models in complex environments. Apart from artifact-centric frameworks, there are also process-centric frameworks that focus on the development process with an analogous aim: to structure these processes in complex environments. Note that the distinction between artifact-centric and process-centric frameworks coincides with the two faces of architecture that we have discussed in Section 2.2.

5.1.1 Zachman framework

One of the best-known architecture design frameworks in practice is the Zachman framework [Zac02, Wi24a], which is a framework for enterprise architecture. Enterprise architecture is a broader concept than (corporate) information system architecture, as it focuses on the organization that forms the context of a (corporate) information system (see also the discussion in Section 2.5). There are several versions of the Zachman framework - we discuss one of them below.

The centerpiece of the Zachman framework is a matrix that intersects six main architecture topics with six groups of stakeholders in the architecture process, as shown in Figure 84. The matrix is used to organize architecture artifacts, i.e., architecture descriptions and models. The six architecture topics are presented as questions labeled with interrogatives: *what, how, where, who, when* and *why*. The stakeholder groups range from people who plan architecture processes to people who are affected by the effects of architecture processes: *planners, owners, designers, builders, implementers* and *workers*.

---

[36] Note that this paper interprets the concept 'framework' in a broader sense than this book does. The Kruchten 4+1 aspect framework (K4+1, see Section 3.2 of this book) and the TOGAF architecture design method (see Section 5.3.3), for example, are taken as frameworks too in the paper. We classify K4+1 as a high-level design approach and TOGAF as a design method.

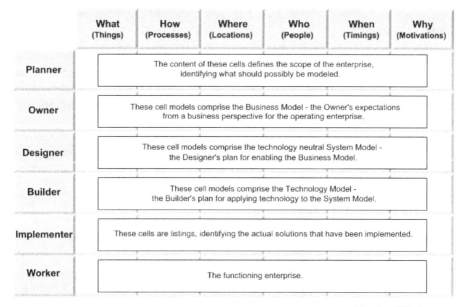

What (Things)	How (Processes)	Where (Locations)	Who (People)	When (Timings)	Why (Motivations)
Planner	The content of these cells defines the scope of the enterprise, identifying what should possibly be modeled.				
Owner	These cell models comprise the Business Model - the Owner's expectations from a business perspective for the operating enterprise.				
Designer	These cell models comprise the technology neutral System Model - the Designer's plan for enabling the Business Model.				
Builder	These cell models comprise the Technology Model - the Builder's plan for applying technology to the System Model.				
Implementer	These cells are listings, identifying the actual solutions that have been implemented.				
Worker	The functioning enterprise.				

Figure 84: Zachman Framework for Enterprise Architecture (taken from [Wi24a])

The stakeholder dimension of the Zachman framework can be related to the realization dimension as discussed in Section 3.4.3, as the groups of stakeholders can be placed along this dimension. Note, however, that the *worker* category is concerned with the functionality of a system described by an architecture, i.e., belongs at the business end of the realization dimension[37]. In other words: the Zachman ordering is a nominal scale (without strict ordering) in this respect, whereas the realization dimension is an ordinal scale (with strict ordering).

The topic dimension of the Zachman framework can be related somewhat to the notion of aspect architectures as discussed in Section 3.2. Note that not all categories can be easily seen as aspects: the *why* category, for example, does not correspond to explicit aspect architecture models. Like the aspect notion, the categories are used to obtain a separation of concerns. The interrogative style of the topic dimension provides an attractive means for this.

---

[37] This observation is based on the assumption that workers have influence on the requirements for the design of a system they will work with (which often is a good approach). If workers are purely seen as users of the technology that results from system design, then the stakeholder dimension of the Zachman framework has an ordinal scale. From this latter point of view, the workers are outside the scope of the realization dimension as discussed in Chapter 3 (as their involvement with the system starts after the realization of the system has been completed).

5.1.2 MDA framework

The Model-Driven Architecture (MDA) framework [Mil01] is an architectural design framework promoted by the Object Management Group (OMG) as a basis for model-driven software engineering[38] [Sch06]. Model-driven software engineering (also referred to as model-driven engineering or MDE) promotes the idea of designing software (and hence also information systems) based on a structural sequence of architecture models that are transformed into each other during the overall design process.

As shown in Figure 85, the MDA framework consists of a number of specification elements (the core), a number of technology elements (the middle ring), a number of application ingredients (the outer ring) and a number of application domains (the outgoing arrows). This figure tries to depict a relation between 'all' aspects relevant in the modern development of distributed information systems – some criticize it for just putting all OMG ideas in a picture.

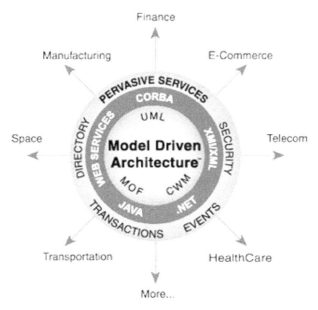

Figure 85: MDA framework (taken from [OM08])

MDA distinguishes between three types of (system aspect) architecture models that play a role in software (and hence information system) development:

---

[38] Model-driven software engineering can be considered a specialization of model-based systems engineering (MBSE). MBSE takes a broader perspective than only software, including also hardware [Bor19].

Computation independent model (CIM): a computation independent model is an architecture model that is independent of any specific computation details; it can be referred to as a business domain model.

Platform independent model (PIM): a platform independent model is an architecture model that is independent of a specific technological platform used to implement it.

Platform specific model (PSM): a platform specific model is an architecture model that is geared towards a specific technological platform.

These three models can be placed along the abstraction dimension (as discussed in Section 3.3), but (indirectly) also along the realization dimension (see Section 3.4.3) as sub-values of the *architecture* value. In MDA, model transformations are proposed as the way to move from a CIM to a PIM and finally to a PSM. A model transformation in this context is a formalized operation that transforms (i.e., structurally translates) a model into another model.

5.2 Architecture specification techniques

To specify architecture models, one requires modeling techniques (typically with specification languages to express them). Often, informal models are used in the 'daily architecture practice'. Though these informal models often seem easily understandable, they typically lack precise semantics: the precise meaning of modeling primitives is undefined. And where models are used for communication, this may (or will) lead to (serious) misunderstandings. And as architecture projects are usually carried out by teams, the use of these informal models may be inconsistent between team members.

Therefore, it is better to use (semi)formal modeling techniques that have well-defined semantics to specify detailed architecture specifications that need to be communicated. And as architectures consist of multiple aspect architectures that each require their own types of specification techniques (as we have seen in Chapter 3 of this book), it is best to choose specification techniques (or sets of aligned techniques) that also address multiple aspects. This means that they allow the specification of various aspects such that all specifications remain compatible with each other.

In this section, we discuss two well-known specification techniques that do address multiple aspects: UML and ArchiMate. There are more architecture specification techniques around, however. See for example [Med00] for a comparison of architecture specification languages.

5.2.1 UML

Probably the most popular specification technique in the information systems domain is the Unified Modeling Language (UML) [Pil05, Mil06, Wi24c]. It was originally developed in the mid-90's at Rational Software. In 1997, it was adopted as a standard by the Object Management Group (OMG) and from that moment managed by this organization. As we have seen in Section 5.1.2, it is for example part of the core of the MDA approach.

UML is a general-purpose modeling language in the field of software engineering, designed to provide a standard way to visualize the design of a system. It is used at various aggregation levels (see Section 3.3) of software design, from small programs to enterprise information systems.

UML Version 2 (UML 2) has many types of diagrams (14, to be precise [Kau18]), which are divided into two categories: *structure diagrams* (with 7 types) and *behavior diagrams* (also with 7 types). Structure diagrams describe static structures of systems. Examples of structure diagrams are *class diagrams*, *component diagrams*, *object diagrams*, and *package diagrams*. Behavior diagrams describe how systems dynamically behave. This category includes diagrams like *use case diagrams*, *activity diagrams*, and *sequence diagrams*.

In this book, we use UML diagrams at various places: Figure 14, Figure 17, and Figure 37 to Figure 39 are UML class diagrams; Figure 15 and Figure 58 are UML component diagrams.

5.2.2 ArchiMate

ArchiMate [Lan05] is an enterprise architecture specification technique (or modeling language) originally developed by a Dutch consortium around the Telematica Instituut (later named Novay) in the Netherlands. Although it originally originated from a background (network architectures) in which other notations techniques are used, it now uses a UML-like notation technique.

ArchiMate offers a common language for describing the construction and operation of business processes, organizational structures, information flows, IT systems, and technical infrastructure [TOG24]. The common language is the basis for a unified way of modeling enterprise architectures consisting of various aspects as we have discussed them in Section 3.2. In ArchiMate, these aspects are called *domains*. The set of ArchiMate domains is different from the set of aspects discussed in Section 3.2. ArchiMate distinguishes a set of domains such as: information, product, process, organization, data, application, and infrastructure [Jon04].

In ArchiMate, services play a central role in the relationships between aspects. Services are organized in three main layers: *business layer*, *application layer*, and *technology layer*. The business layer contains products and services offered to external parties, realized by business processes. The application layer contains the application services that support the business layer. These application services are realized by software components. The technology layer contains infrastructural services required to run the application services[39].

A simple insurance claim architecture in ArchiMate with the three layers indicated is shown in Figure 86. In the business layer, we see the business process that is triggered by a damage notification. The three steps in the process each use a service in the application layer, which uses an underlying information system that implements its functionality. The information systems use the infrastructure in the technology layer. In Chapter 6 of this book, we discuss the differences between application and infrastructure layers in a more general sense in more detail.

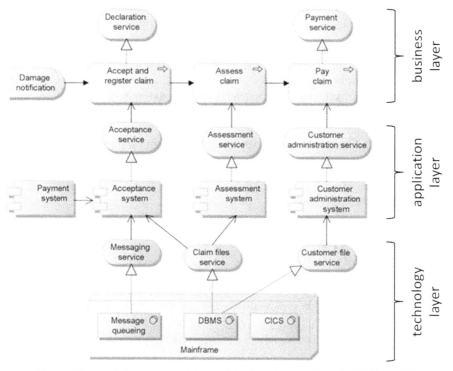

Figure 86: simple insurance claim architecture in ArchiMate (extended from [Wi24j])

ArchiMate is an Open Group standard [TOG24], supported by different vendors of modeling tools and consulting firms. Its specification describes relationships with other methods and techniques, such as the Zachman framework (see Section 5.1.1) and TOGAF (see Section 5.4.1). In 2016, ArchiMate 3.0 was released by the Open Group [TOG16]. The most recent version at the time of writing this book is ArchiMate 3.1 [TOG24, Wie21].

---

[39] The technology layer corresponds with what we describe as *infrastructure* in Chapter 6

.

5.3 Architecture design approaches

In this chapter so far, we have discussed architecture frameworks and architecture specification techniques. These ingredients of architecture provide a general context for thinking about architecture processes respectively ways to specify architecture models. They do not describe (or prescribe) how to actually perform an architecture design process. As we have seen in Chapter 3 of this book, the K4+1 framework can be considered a high-level architecture design approach, as it describes a sequence of design views. But this framework provides no further guidelines for an architecture design approach. Therefore, we address this topic here.

In the next section, we discuss architecture design methods as 'design recipes', which can be considered concrete design approaches. As a stepping stone to these methods, we pay attention in this section to considerations that influence architecture design processes in practice. We do this from three perspectives. First, we pay attention to *top-down* versus *bottom-up* architecture design. Next, we discuss how the distinction between several *architecture aspects* can influence an architecture design process. Then, we discuss the relation between *agile system development* and architecture.

5.3.1 Top-down versus bottom-up design

An architecture design is best made in a situation unconstrained by choices made in the past – often referred to as a *greenfield situation*. In this kind of situation, one can make a strictly top-down design, i.e., go down the aggregation dimension in well-chosen steps. Doing so, one starts with the 'grand picture' and gradually adds more detail. In going down the aggregation dimension, one can traverse also the abstraction and realization dimension, much like we have seen the ways to work through the architecture cube in Section 3.6. A top-down design process can be a good basis to ensure consistency between sub-architectures.

In most practical situations, however, an architect is confronted with an existing situation that often is of a nature that is far from ideal (as discussed before in Section 2.1) – often referred to as a *legacy situation*. If one would apply a strict top-down design here, one might make choices that do not fit the structure of the existing situation. This does not only concern the existing architecture, which could be redrawn, but more importantly the existing information systems that embody the architecture, which cannot be changed that easily. This implies that an architect typically must design in a 'hybrid' way: in a bottom-up fashion from what already exists and in a top-down fashion from what is wanted. In terms of the architecture cube of Section 3.6, this means that the starting point of the design may partly be somewhere 'in the middle' of the cube. This hybrid approach may need to have an iterative character to get everything consistent.

5.3.2 Dealing with aspects

In Section 3.2, we have discussed the concept of aspect and aspect architecture. When designing an architecture, one is confronted with the question when to design which aspect architectures in the overall design process.

Ideally, all aspects can be treated independently. This means that one could start a design process with an informal global design paying attention to a few major aspects, then design all aspects in parallel, and end up with an overview model highlighting only the major aspects again. This is illustrated in Figure 87, where the circles and ovals denote aspects, and two major aspects are taken as starting and ending point in the process.

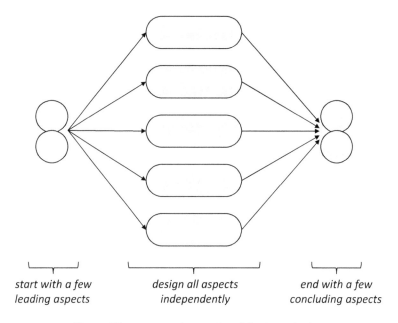

| start with a few | design all aspects | end with a few |
| leading aspects | independently | concluding aspects |

Figure 87: concurrent aspect architecture design

Apart from the fact that it is not always practical to do all in parallel (as it requires a lot of manpower), this approach has one potential problem: in practice, the aspects are usually not completely independent (as illustrated by the arrows in the graphical representation of the UT5 framework). This means that if inconsistent aspect architectures are designed, this only becomes apparent at the integration phase at the end (at the right of Figure 87).

To avoid this, one may use a phased approach as illustrated in Figure 88. Here, the aspect architectures are designed sequentially (but possibly overlapping in time, as shown in the figure). This means that design choices taken for one aspect architecture can be taken into account in the following aspect architectures. Starting with the aspects with the most critical design choices will lead to the best chances of a consistent overall architecture design. The downside of this phased approach is obvious: the entire design process takes longer. The less the design steps for the individual aspects overlap, the more room there is for handling dependencies between aspect architectures, but the more time is needed to complete the entire process.

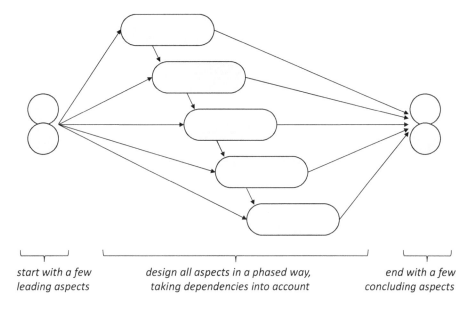

start with a few   design all aspects in a phased way,   end with a few
leading aspects   taking dependencies into account   concluding aspects

Figure 88: phased aspect architecture design

5.3.3 Agile system development

A relatively new approach to information system development is *agile development*. The basis of this approach is the idea that development of complex software should be performed in small, incremental steps that are guided by dynamically evolving requirements. *Scrum* is a well-known approach for agile information system (or general software) development.

Scrum is in principle a domain-independent framework for structuring the iterative development of complex products [Scr11]. Although the framework is domain-independent, it has been advocated for the software development domain. Scrum tries to combine agility in development with strict project management. The basis of Scrum is the idea that product development is organized in strictly time-boxed development periods (called 'sprints' in Scrum lingo). The development is based on requirements that are specified in an explicitly managed, dynamically evolving requirement list ('the product backlog'). The product backlog is extended by developments in markets and reduced by executing sprints. Scrum strictly dictates a number of roles in the development process with clearly defined responsibilities. Scrum does not prescribe any design or specification techniques. As it is a process framework, techniques can be chosen depending on the context in which Scrum is applied.

Often, agile development and architecture-based development are seen in practice as two approaches that are opposed to each other, as agile development relies on *adaptation* and architecture-based development on *anticipation* [Abr10]. Agile development methods suggest to decide things at the last possible moment during the software development process to take evolving requirements into consideration, which can lead to system structures that 'emerge' in the process. Architecture-based development approaches suggest to decide on all important structures before the actual software development process starts, which leads to 'predefined' system structures. Agile development and architecture-based development can be combined productively in practice, however [Abr10]. Architecture thinking can provide a structural framework, in which agile development can be embedded, leading to *agile architecture* [Mad10].

5.4 Architecture design methods

Given all the previous considerations in this chapter, we now turn briefly to architecture design methods. Design methods are meant to be standardized descriptions (or prescriptions) of architecture design processes. As such they typically specify:

- the steps to take in an architecture design process, including their order;

- the documents to produce in each of the steps, containing the architecture models (the deliverables);

- the stakeholders to involve in each step with their respective responsibilities.

Below, we briefly discuss two example methods: one well-known example from the business domain (that has been used in many large projects) and one 'simpler' example that has emerged from the academic domain (that has been used in research and teaching contexts).

5.4.1 TOGAF ADM

The Open Group Architecture Framework (TOGAF) [TOG07, TOG15] is a detailed framework, method and a set of supporting design tools for developing enterprise architectures and information system architectures. It has developed since the mid 1990's by members of The Open Group Architecture Forum (www.opengroup.org/architecture). By many, it is considered as *the standard* in architecture design frameworks.

The Architecture Development Method (ADM) is the core of the TOGAF framework. It describes a method for developing and managing the lifecycle of enterprise architecture [Wi24d].

TOGAF is a high-level approach to architecture design. The approach typically uses four levels of models [Wi24d]: *business*, *application*, *data*, and *technology*. It relies heavily on modularization, standardization, and already existing, proven technologies and products.

5.4.2 COMET

COMET (Component and Model-based development Methodology) [Ber06] is a use case-driven, model-focused approach for developing and maintaining software products and software product families. COMET is UML-based in its specification techniques. The method was originally developed by a team of researchers from Norway and the UK in the COMBINE research project and used in architecture teaching.

In COMET, we find four types of models [Ber06]:

- the *business model*, which includes goals, business processes, steps within business processes, roles and resources.

- the *requirements model*, which identifies the requirements to the system under development, including functional requirements, non-functional requirements (quality of service) and constraints.

- the *architecture model*, which describes the overall architecture of the system and its partitioning into components in terms of collaborations of components and subsystems, component structures, component interactions, and component interfaces and protocols.

- the *platform specific model*, which defines the result of mapping the component model (as part of the architecture model) to an implementation on a particular infrastructure.

5.5 Architecture principles

Architecture principles are typically general laws or 'rules of thumb' that can be applied in the design of information system architectures. They can have various appearances, ranging from the more formal to the very informal, but often they have a strong practical character.

Architecture design principles are related to software design principles. Software design principles are targeted more at the level of software engineering, however, where we focus on information system engineering (see the discussion in Section 2.5). But the aim of both types of principles are similar: to improve the quality of the systems under design. For example, Kandt defines a software design principle as follows [Kan03]:

A software design principle is a comprehensive and fundamental doctrine or rule that governs the creation of quality software designs.

An architecture principle can relate to architecture as a product or architecture as a process (as discussed in Section 2.2). Architecture principles can be related to methods, like TOGAF ADM [Gre11].

Architecture principles can be found in isolation, in sets, or in extensive catalogs. Obviously, catalogs provide most structure for practical use, as they allow architects to find the most applicable principles for a specific design project. We discuss one such catalog below as an example.

5.5.1 Greefhorst and Proper catalog

Greefhorst and Proper have devoted an entire book to the topic of architecture principles for the design of enterprise information systems [Gre11]. They define the concept of architecture principle as follows:

A design principle included in an architecture. As such, it is a declarative statement that normatively prescribes a property of the design of an artifact, which is necessary to ensure that the artifact meets its essential requirements.

In this context, an artifact is typically an architecture model (as we have seen in many forms in this book), but may also be a system resulting from an architecting process.

The book by Greefhorst and Proper includes a catalog of 59 architecture principles. Each principle is described using a template that includes the formulation of the principle plus a specification of the type of information for the principle, the architecture quality attributes addressed by the principle, the rationale for the principle and the implications of the principle.

An (arbitrary) example architecture principle specification from the catalog in the book is shown in Figure 89. This principle highlights the importance of standardization in application (i.e., information system or part thereof) development.

A.57 Application Development Is Standardized

Type of information: application

Quality attributes: reliability. maintainability

Rationale:

- Application development is labor intensive. error prone and relatively costly.
- The business should focus time. money. people and knowledge on business innovations.

Implications:

- Software development standards and guidelines exist.
- Standard software factories. based on software generation techniques are employed.
- Declarative techniques are used for defining logic. such as business rule and process languages.

Figure 89: example architecture principle from a catalog of principles [from [Gre11]]

6

DISTINGUISHING BETWEEN APPLICATIONS AND INFRASTRUCTURES

In this chapter, we discuss the important difference between applications and infrastructures in the architecture field. Applications are information (software) systems that support specific business functions. They are designed with specific business goals in mind and determine what an organization can do. Infrastructures are information (software) systems that provide general-purpose functionality that can be used across business functions – usually to support applications. Hence, they are designed from a more general point of view. They do not directly determine what an organization can do in functional terms but can determine how applications work in non-functional terms (like performance or availability).

One can use a railroad analogy to explain the difference between applications and infrastructure: the infrastructure in a specific context (e.g. an organization) can be compared to the railroad tracks of a railway system, whereas the applications can be compared to the trains deployed (riding) on the infrastructure (as illustrated in Figure 90). The trains determine what a railroad can do from a functional perspective, like transport passengers or transport specific kinds of freight. The tracks provide the support needed to drive trains and are not directly related to what a train transports. The tracks do determine non-functional aspects, though, like the maximum speed at which trains can run.

Figure 90: applications and infrastructure paraphrased:
trains on tracks at Maastricht Central Station (photo by author)

In this chapter, we first discuss the concepts and the layering of applications and infrastructure. Then, we pay attention to the structures of application and infrastructure elements for business information systems. After that, we go into the relation between application and infrastructure architecture processes.

6.1 Application and infrastructure layers

In this section, we analyze the layering of application and infrastructure elements in an information system architecture landscape. We first discuss the principle of layering and the concept of a layer stack. Next, we relate the topic to the concept of multi-tier architecture.

6.1.1 Layering applications and infrastructure

Application software systems make use of the functions of infrastructure software systems. The application layer contains the logic (implemented in software) of specific business functions connected to the user interface layer. We discuss the elements of the application layer in Section 6.2. The infrastructure layer contains general-purpose functionality that is not specific to business functions and can hence be used by multiple application systems. We discuss the elements in the infrastructure layer in Section 6.3. The infrastructure layer itself uses functionality of operating system software, which again uses hardware functions. The overall layering is shown in Figure 91. Obviously, the

132

structure of the layering is related to the layered architecture style as discussed in Section 4.1.3 – but here, we use it in a broad perspective.

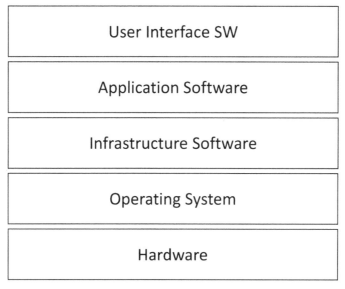

Figure 91: application and infrastructure layers in context

In layered architectures like the one shown in Figure 91, we often use the concept of *platform*. A platform for a specific layer is the functionality offered by the layers beneath that specific layer. For example, the platform for the infrastructure software in Figure 91 is the combination of operating system and underlying hardware. Note that the term *platform* in this context is related to the term *platform* in the context of the UT5 aspect model (as discussed in Section 3.2.3), but it is not exactly the same. Here, the concept *platform* refers to a part of a software stack and thereby dissects this software stack. The entire software stack is reflected in the *software* and *platform* aspects the UT5 model, where the *software* aspect covers what is explicitly under design, and the *platform* aspect covers what is assumed to be available. In other words, the UT5 distinction dissects the design goals.

6.1.2 Relation to multi-tier architectures

The layered model that distinguishes between application and infrastructure (Figure 91) can be compared with other layered models that are used in the information system architecture domain.

Two well-known models are the three-tier and four-tier architecture models, which are both realizations of the layered architecture style (see Section 4.1). A four-tier architecture consists of four layers (referred to as tiers), as shown on the right side in Figure 92:

- The presentation logic tier contains the logic that implements the interaction with the human user of information systems.

- The process logic tier contains the logic that implements the process flow (workflow) between the individual tasks that an information system supports.

- The business logic tier contains the logic that implements the individual business functions that an information system supports.

- The data logic tier contains the logic that implements the operations on the business data that is used by the business logic tier.

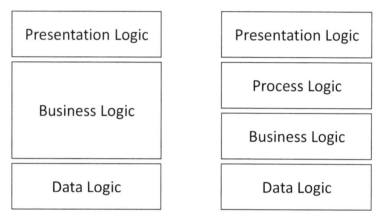

Figure 92: 3-tier (left) and 4-tier (right) architecture structures

A 3-tier structure (shown on the left in Figure 92) typically does not include the process logic tier. In the 3-tier structure, process aspects are considered part of the business logic. The business logic thus becomes more complex, with an inherent risk of decreased modularity of the logic. In the spectrum of multi-tiered models, also service-oriented variants exist. An example is the service-oriented multi-tier reference architecture that is part of the COMET information system design method [Ber06]. The SOA reference architecture of The Open Group shown in Figure 78 can also be considered a multi-tier architecture (with five tiers).

Multi-tier architectures can raise the impression that all tiers have to be realized in one project, i.e., within the scope of the development of one single information system. This may lead to the development of process logic and data logic including supporting software that is specific for one information system and hence cannot be shared with other information systems. To paraphrase in terms of the railroad example from the beginning of this chapter: the development of a new train may lead to the development of new railroads built only for this one specific train. This is a process that is often referred to as 'silo forming': each information system exists in each own vertical silo.

We can avoid this problem by distinguishing between the application-specific process and data logic on the one hand (at a higher level of aggregation), and general-purpose process and data logic on the other hand (at a lower level of aggregation). The application-specific logic uses the general-purpose logic for basic operations concerning process and data management. These basic operations are performed in this case by general-purpose (COTS) business process management systems and database management systems that are part of the infrastructure layer. We show this in Figure 93 for both the 3-tier and 4-tier structure.

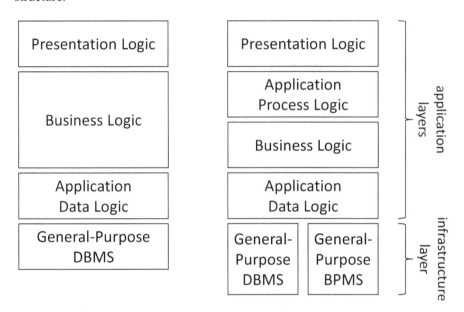

Figure 93: 3-tier and 4-tier structures with infrastructure layer

6.2 Application layer elements

The application layer consists of the interconnected information system components that together support the business operation of an organization (i.e., the business logic, and the application-specific process and data logic, as we have seen in the previous section). In other words: the application layer contains the main functional elements of a (corporate) information system and the connections between these.

6.2.1 Modularization of the application layer

A main task of an architect in the design of an application layer is to establish the modularization of its functionality, i.e., to establish which functional elements to distinguish in the application layer architecture. Note that even when an overall list of functionalities of the system exists, various modularizations are possible because of various possible ways of grouping these functionalities (i.e., using multiple possible bottom-up aggregations – see Section 3.3). An optimal modularization is essential to support adequate maintainability of systems: too few modules may create rigidity with respect to evolution of the functionality of systems, too many modules may create unnecessary complexity and hence overhead in both maintenance and operation of systems.

To identify the main functional elements in an application layer architecture, one can use a generally accepted operational business model framework. This framework can be the basis for the modularization. Using a generally accepted framework provides 'reference value' and prevents thinking too much in the 'here and now' of an organization. Below, we show how Porter's value chain model can be used for this purpose (other business framework models can be used similarly).

6.2.2 Porter's value chain model

Porter's value chain model [Por85] is a model of a business organization highlighting its main business functions. An adapted version of the model is shown in Figure 94.

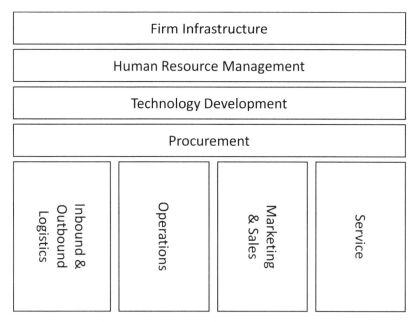

Figure 94: adapted version of Porter's value chain model

The model distinguishes between two classes of business functions: primary functions and secondary functions. Primary functions are directly geared towards the main business goal of the organization: the production and delivery of goods. Secondary functions support the primary functions by providing a necessary context to execute the primary functions.

The primary functions are shown as the four vertical columns in the bottom half of Figure 94. The *inbound & outbound logistics* function[40] enables the transport of materials used as input in production, respectively the transport of produced goods to consumers of these goods. The *operations* function performs the actual production of goods. The *marketing & sales* function takes care of attracting these customers and arranging the actual sales. Finally, the *services* function is responsible for after-sales service to customers.

The secondary functions are shown as the four horizontal layers in the top half of Figure 94. The *procurement* function takes care of ordering the goods and services required in the other functions (most importantly the *operations* function). As its name suggests, the *technology development* function concentrates on the development of new technologies used in the *operations* function or in the produced goods. The *human resource management* function manages the personnel of the organization. Finally, the *firm infrastructure* function is responsible for providing the general infrastructure of the organization, such as the (financial) administration.

Porter's value chain model was originally designed for organizations that handle and produce physical materials (like factories). With a little abstraction, however, the model can also be used for other business domains. For example, in the financial domain, the *operations* function creates financial services and needs financial input (via the *inbound logistics* function) and distributes the created services (via the *outbound logistics* function).

6.2.3 An application layer structure

Taking the business function structure described above and shown in Figure 94, we can design an application layer modules structure as shown in Figure 95 (where the infrastructure layer is shown and the user interface layer is omitted for clarity).

The entire architecture in Figure 95 has a layered style with two layers: the application layer and the infrastructure layer (see Section 4.1.2). Embedded in this layered style is a clear example of a sub-architecture with a columned style. For the application layer, separation of concerns based on a business function model (in this case Porter's model) is used to arrive at a columned organization of this layer.

---

[40] Note that Porter's original value chain model [Por85] describes the inbound and outbound logistics function as two separate functions. We have combined them as they require similar information systems support.

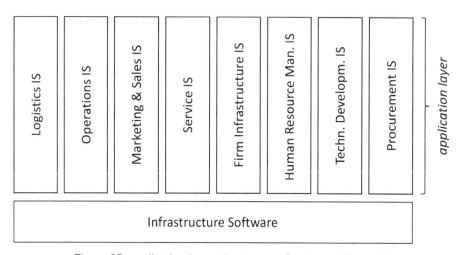

Figure 95: application layer structure conforming to Figure 94
on top of infrastructure layer

Within each of the application layer columns, individual concrete information system components can be distinguished, as illustrated in Figure 96. In other words, we can go down the aggregation dimension (as discussed in Section 3.3) within a column. For instance, the Human Resources Management (HRM) IS column may contain a Personnel Information System, a Salary System, a Training Administration System and a Personnel Planning System as shown in Figure 96. To not clutter things in the figure, we have detailed only one column in this architecture – the other columns can be elaborated in a similar way by identifying the individual systems in these columns.

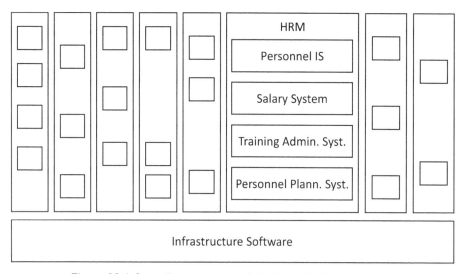

Figure 96: information system modules in application columns,
with HRM column detailed

For a second example case, we can return to the TOA OMIS airline information system that we have introduced in Chapter 3 (see Figure 28). There, we have seen an information system for operations management with six subsystems. This overall information system can be mapped to the Operations IS column of Figure 95, and the six subsystems can be mapped to systems within this column. This leads to the architecture in Figure 97 (again with only one column detailed to not clutter things).

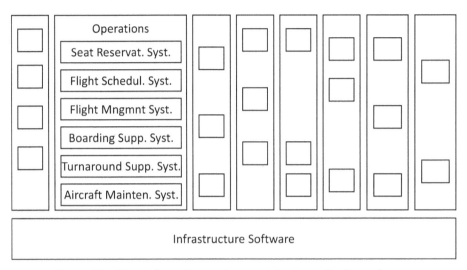

Figure 97: airline information system modules in application columns, with Operations column detailed

As an airline also has an HRM business function (as it does employ personnel), the HRM column in Figure 97 might be detailed as shown in Figure 96. This shows the power of modularity in architecture design: an airline may want to have a specific design for its operations system (as this supports the primary process of the airline and hence needs to be tuned to its specific value proposition to customers) but may use a standard design for its HRM system (as this supports a secondary process). Obviously, in business architecture practice, all columns need to be elaborated. For reasons of brevity, we skip this exercise in this chapter.

6.3 Infrastructure layer elements

The infrastructure layer consists of the interconnected software system modules that together support the functionality of the application layer. In other words: the infrastructure layer contains the main supportive elements of a business information system and the connections between these.

6.3.1 Modularization of the infrastructure layer

Like in the case of the application layer, a main design aspect of the infrastructure layer architecture is its modularization, i.e., determining which elements to distinguish between.

The infrastructure layer elements are not defined by a business function classification, but by a general support functionality classification. There are no generally accepted frameworks here (such as the Porter framework for the application layer), but there are generally recognized support functionalities that can be used as the basis for a classification that has the function of a framework. We discuss this classification below.

6.3.2 Support system classification

We can compose a support system classification based on general information system support functions. A very simple classification of important support functions is:

- Business data management: typically performed by means of a database management system (DBMS) [Elm10] – the most important class for business applications being the relational database management system (RDBMS).

- Business process management: typically performed by a business process management system (BPMS) or workflow management system (WFMS) [Ley99]. In organizations with flexible processes, dynamic case management systems [Kar24] may be used as an alternative.

- System interoperability support: typically performed by middleware systems that are designed to interconnect other systems in heterogeneous and distributed environments. An example of a middleware system is an enterprise service bus (ESB) [Cha04]. We discuss middleware in Chapter 9 of this book.

The above classification can be extended (add classes) and refined (specialize classes). For example, the business data management class can be refined into the subclasses online transaction processing (OLTP) support and online analytical processing (OLAP) support [Sin21].

6.3.3 An infrastructure layer structure

An example structure of a simple infrastructure layer supporting an application layer is shown in Figure 98. Here, we see that a bus (like an enterprise service bus) for system interoperability support is used to interconnect both the other infrastructure elements to each other and the infrastructure elements to the application layer elements (and often even to connect the application layer elements to each other). The application layer elements make use of the functions of the infrastructure layer elements via this bus.

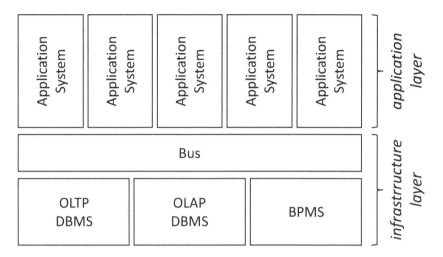

Figure 98: infrastructure layer structure (bottom two layers) supporting application layer (top layer)

Typically, one application layer element can make use of multiple infrastructure layer elements (an application system, for example, may use a DBMS and a BPMS). One infrastructure layer element may be used by multiple application layer elements (e.g., one DBMS can manage the databases of multiple application systems). Hence, the relation between application layer elements and infrastructure layer elements is *m:n*. Middleware (like the bus in Figure 98) helps in managing this *m:n* relation, as we explain in detail in Chapter 9 of this book.

6.4 Application and infrastructure architecting processes

Often, the application layer and infrastructure layer are treated separately from an architecture process point of view. This separate treatment is caused by the different lifecycles of the two layers as we explain below. This may even lead to the distinction between the roles of application architect and infrastructure architect as we see further on in this section.

6.4.1 Application and infrastructure lifecycles

The functionality of an application layer is typically determined by the business functions that it should support. Consequently, an application layer architecture is typically changed when business functions of an organization change. This means that an application layer architecture lifecycle to a large extent is determined by *requirements pull* forces (as discussed in Section 2.1.5).

The functionality of an infrastructure layer does not typically change when business functions in the application layer change (as the infrastructure functions are general-purpose and hence applicable to various business functions). The architecture of an infrastructure layer may, however, change when new infrastructure systems with different structures become available. Thus, an infrastructure layer architecture lifecycle is heavily influenced by *technology push* forces (as discussed in Section 2.1.5).

Consequently, the architectures of the application layer and of the infrastructure layer evolve at their own paces. Often, an infrastructure architecture changes at a lower frequency than an application architecture. The different paces of evolution should not cause great problems in a well-designed overall architecture (as illustrated in Figure 11). In a badly designed overall architecture, however, they can cause serious headaches.

6.4.2 Economics of applications and infrastructures

As discussed above, application architectures are typically related to functional requirements for specific business function support systems. This can imply that an application architecture design is heavily governed by direct cost/benefit considerations related to the business functions that will be supported by the system(s) described in the architecture. A new (or redesigned) system may be essential for the realization of a new (or redesigned) business function of an organization, which is aimed at directly generating new revenue for that organization.

Cost/benefit considerations (obviously) also play a role in the design of infrastructure architectures (and the design of the systems described by them), but these considerations are often not directly related to specific business functions. A new database management platform may for example be described by a new infrastructure architecture. This platform will enhance data processing in general but will not directly generate new revenue for an organization. This means that it is often harder to make a cost/benefit analysis for redesigning an infrastructure architecture and consequently adapting the systems that it describes. This may lead to postponing the modernization of the infrastructure architecture of an organization and consequently the emergence of a legacy problem (as discussed in Section 2.1.3).

6.4.3 Application and infrastructure architects

As application architectures and infrastructure architectures each evolve at their own pace, many large organizations allocate specialized architects to each of the two architecture layers (as illustrated in Figure 99). Consequently, we see two architect roles in these organizations: application architects and infrastructure architects.

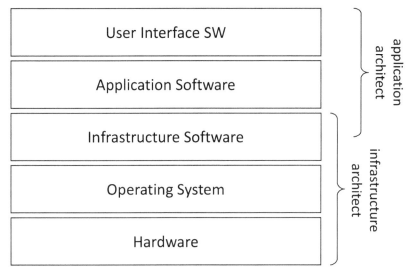

Figure 99: architects and layers

An application architect is concerned with the business functionality of systems. This function is closely related to that of an enterprise architect – in some organizations, these functions are treated similar, in some the enterprise architect makes the abstract, business-oriented designs and the application architect maps these to system structures.

An infrastructure architect is concerned with the digital infrastructure that supports the business applications. In some organizations, this function is called technical architect. Typically, an infrastructure architect deals with non-functional requirements of overall corporate digital systems, like performance, availability, and scalability.

As the infrastructure layer must support the application layer, one may conclude that application architects set the scene for infrastructure architects, i.e., they are the leading role. Though correct from a very general point of view, this is not completely the case for two main reasons:

- Given the scope and complexity of modern digital infrastructures (supporting intra-organizational application integration, inter-organizational application integration, mobile applications, ubiquitous computing, advanced security, etcetera), the architecture of this layer cannot always be completely controlled from an application point of view.

- One infrastructure typically serves multiple applications, each possibly having its own architect(s) assigned. Applications may have different (and even conflicting) requirements to the infrastructure layer. This means that infrastructure architects may have to reconcile demands of multiple application architects.

So mostly, we see a more intricate interaction between (teams of) application architects and infrastructure architects. Often this interaction is both of a project-based nature (to align architectures when major changes to business information systems are needed) and a periodic nature (to align in a more general sense and discuss general architecture strategies towards the future). In complex organizations, it may be a good idea to appoint one or several senior architects that are responsible for keeping the teams of application architects and infrastructure architects well-aligned.

7 ARCHITECTURES OF CONCRETE SYSTEMS

In the preceding six chapters of this book, we have discussed many aspects and elements of business information system architecture. Even though we have illustrated these with many examples, the emphasis in these chapters is on abstract concepts of architecture, not on architecture of concrete systems. To provide a complementary point of view, we discuss architectures of concrete systems in this chapter.

The purpose of this chapter is not to be complete, but rather to provide a discussion of the architecture of a number of system classes to highlight their structuring principles with some practical aspects. We discuss the following architectures in this chapter:

- A data warehousing architecture, both on the reference architecture level and at the concrete system level.

- A business process management architecture, both on the reference architecture level and at the concrete system level.

- An application system architecture, only at the concrete system level (because a general reference architecture is not available here). We do however pay extra attention to interoperability patterns (as discussed in Section 4.2) here.

7.1 Data warehousing architecture

In this section, we discuss an enterprise-level architecture for data warehousing, i.e., for managing data that is used in business intelligence. Large organizations typically employ data warehouses for this purpose: central storages of all data potentially relevant as a basis for management information, i.e., all data that can serve as input for tactic and strategic decision making. Sometimes, data warehouses are also used for high-level operational decision making, but this requires fast processing of data into and from a data warehouse. A data warehouse is often referred to as 'the single point of truth' for decision making. This means that it contains an agreed-upon, consistent state of data for decision making.

Data warehouses for business intelligence are of a very different nature than operational database systems that directly serve the execution of business processes for a number of reasons:

- Data warehouses usually contain abstracted/aggregated data, because for tactical/strategic decision making, not all operational details are necessary; operational databases must contain all details (for OLTP).

- Data in warehouses is not updated like in operational databases, as it reflects 'the truth' at a point in time – data is only extended with new facts. When necessary (e.g., for storage limitations), old data can be archived from a data warehouse to an off-line storage.

- Historic data is important in data warehouses to enable trend analysis. For this reason, data is commonly time-stamped. In operational databases, data about the 'here and now' is usually most important.

- Data warehouse systems typically have very different performance requirements than operational database systems: warehouses must be able to run complex queries where response time is not of prime importance, where operational database systems usually execute small transactions with strict response time requirements.

Below, we first discuss a reference architecture for data warehousing that can be used as a general architectural blueprint for the context of this class of systems. Next, we apply this reference architecture in a concrete example scenario from the airline industry.

7.1.1 Reference architecture

A general reference architecture for data warehousing in an enterprise setting is shown in Figure 100. In this architecture, we see the data warehouse as a central component in the middle. This component is the centralized storage for data to be processed into management information. On the left of the data warehouse, we find components that are responsible for getting data into the warehouse -

the input side. On the right of the data warehouse, we find components that use data stored in the warehouse (typically, data is not removed for use, but just copied) - the output side.

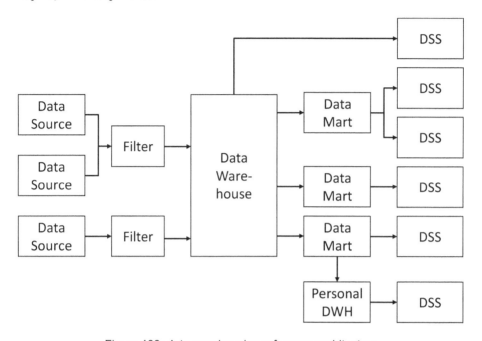

Figure 100: data warehousing reference architecture

The input side of the architecture contains data source components and filter components. Data source components are typically operational information systems, i.e., information systems used in the operational business processes of an organization (i.e., OLTP systems). These systems contain all the data about what is happening 'on the work floor' of an organization. There may also be external data sources providing data on what is happening outside the organization.

The filter components are responsible for transferring data from the data sources into the data warehouse. This copying involves selecting the relevant data, transforming it where so required, and cleaning the data. Transforming can include aggregating, normalizing, and anonymizing. Cleaning can include removing faulty data and repairing inconsistent data. In general, operational data always goes through a filter before added to a central data warehouse – this keeps the quality of data high.

On the output side of the architecture we find the decision support systems (DSSs). These are the systems used by the people (or systems) that make the tactic or strategic (and sometimes operational decisions). The DSSs can range from simple management dashboards to complex analytical tools (often referred to as OLAP engines, where OLAP is the acronym for OnLine Analytical Processing).

DSS components can be decoupled from the central data warehouse by the use of smaller data warehouses, called data marts (used for example by a specific department within an organization) or personal data warehouses (used by a single employee). There are several potential reasons for this decoupling. A first reason is efficiency: if many DSSs are connected to a single data warehouse, the load for the central warehouse system may get too high. Therefore, work is distributed over the smaller warehouses. A second reason is security: if not all decision makers can have access to all data in the central data warehouse, giving them a copy of a part of the warehouse solves this issue. A third reason is modification: if decision makers want the make changes to data in the data warehouse (for example to perform a what-if analysis on corporate data), then this is preferably done on a copy of the data - this to not mess up the central data warehouse.

From the above discussion, we can deduce that there are a number of stages in data processing in a data warehousing architecture. This means that we can make 'functional slices' of the architecture, which either suggests a layered or a columned architecture style (as discussed in Section 4.1). As this 'slicing' is more a separation of concerns than a layering of abstraction levels, this is clearly a columned architecture. This is illustrated in Figure 101, where we can see five columns. The column containing the input filters is commonly referred to as *extraction and transformation logic* (ETL).

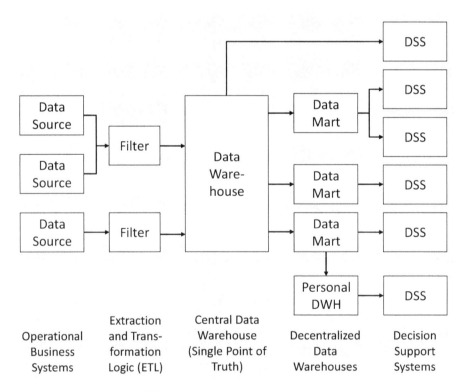

Figure 101: DW reference architecture in a columned style

Note that an architecture with three columns would have been possible too: input side, data warehouse, output side. This is a matter of architecture organization - the preference depends on the purpose of the architecture.

7.1.2 Concrete architecture

We apply the reference architecture for data warehousing from the previous subsection in the design of a concrete architecture of the international airline company *Trans-Oceanic Airways* (TOA) that we have seen before in this book.

TOA's high-level data warehousing architecture is shown in Figure 102. TOA has decided to organize the overall data warehousing architecture in three columns by merging two pairs of columns of Figure 101: data sources, central data warehouse management, and application areas.

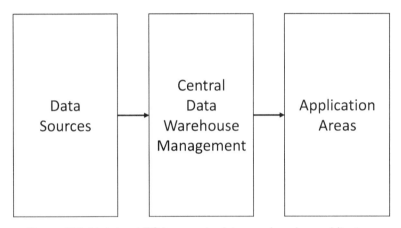

Figure 102: high-level TOA concrete data warehousing architecture

The data sources column of Figure 102 is refined into two sub-columns:

- internal operations support sources;
- external sources.

The application areas column is refined into five sub-columns:

- three sub-columns are dedicated to business in their geographic business areas: Europe/Middle East/Africa (EMEA), Americas, and Asia/Oceania;
- one sub-column supports global flight planning;
- one sub-column supports global strategy development.

The sub-columns contain component systems following the reference architecture in Figure 101. This results in the concrete, detailed architecture of Figure 103. Note that the two sets of sub-columns are shown in a vertical arrangement, but they are columns from a functional point of view. Hence, the architecture in Figure 103 is a two-level columned architecture (see the discussion on architecture styles in Section 4.1).

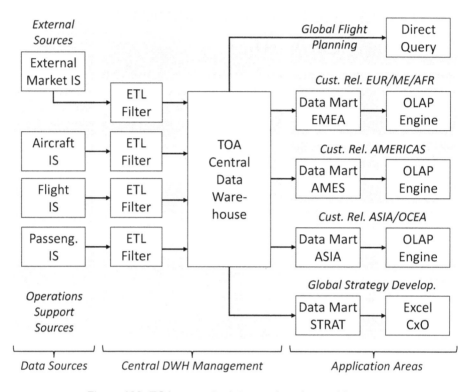

Figure 103: TOA concrete data warehousing architecture

On the input side, we find three internal data source components: the aircraft database system, the flight database system, and the passenger database system. These three systems contain the main operating data of TOA. Next to these, there is one external source that provides global market data. Each of the data sources is coupled to the central warehouse via a dedicated filter component with ETL functionality. The filter for the passenger information system, for example, anonymizes passenger data, such that privacy of customers is not violated in business intelligence. The filter for the aircraft database removes all technical information of aircraft that is not used for business decision making in TOA.

On the output side, we see five DSS systems. There is one centralized, global flight planning DSS, which is used by TOA to compose their flight schedules. As this system requires access to all data in the warehouse, it is directly connected to the warehouse through a query interface. Three DSS systems are used for customer relationship management (CRM) and marketing. These systems use OLAP engines. As TOA operates in three regions with their own CRM and marketing strategies, they have decided to create local data marts for each region. These three data marts are periodically fed with data from the central warehouse that concerns their regions. Finaly, there is a data mart for global strategy development. From this data mart, Excel spreadsheets are generated for the offices of various global managers, such as the COO and CFO. These spreadsheets allow performing what-if analyses in a user-friendly way.

7.2 Business process management architecture

In this section, we pay attention to architectures for business process management (BPM). First, we discuss two reference architectures for BPM environments: WfMC and Mercurius. The WfMC architecture has a mostly industrial origin, the Mercurius architecture a mostly academic origin. Then, we discuss an application of one of these architectures in a concrete business context in the insurance domain.

7.2.1 WfMC reference architecture

The best-known architecture for business process management systems is the reference architecture promoted by the Workflow Management Coalition (WfMC) [Hol95]. We have already briefly discussed this in Section 4.3 and show it again in Figure 104. In this context, workflow management is synonymous to business process management (the latter is a more contemporary term, though).

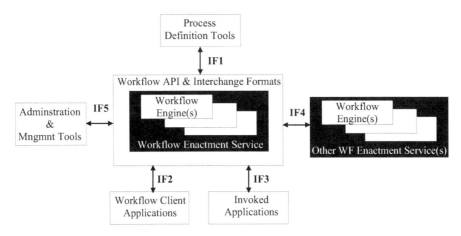

Figure 104: WfMC reference architecture for workflow management systems

The heart of the WfMC architecture is the workflow enactment service. This service consists of one or more workflow engines. A workflow engine is a software module that can interpret a workflow (business process) specification and execute it by having the right actors (or automated systems) perform the right tasks at the right time with the right information. As shown in the architecture, the workflow enactment service is wrapped in an interface layer. The interface layer connects the enactment service to five classes of other modules through interfaces 1 to 5 (designated as IF1 to IF5 in the architecture).

The first class of modules contains the process definition tools. These are used to compose a workflow specification that can be interpreted by the enactment service (using IF1). The second class contains the workflow client applications, connected via IF2. These are the interactive software modules that are used to allocate tasks to human actors and support them in executing these tasks. Comparably, IF3 links the enactment service to automated applications that are invoked to perform tasks in a workflow. IF4 is the link to other enactment services such that distributed workflow management environments can be created. Finally, the module set connected through IF5 contains the administration and management tools that support the operational management of the enactment service. Through these tools, actors can be added or deleted, priorities can be set, back-ups can be made, et cetera.

7.2.2 Mercurius reference architecture

In Section 4.3.2, we have seen the Mercurius reference architecture for business process management systems [Gre98] as an alternative to the WfMC reference architecture. As mentioned there, the Mercurius architecture is defined at three aggregation levels. In Section 4.3.2, we have already seen two of these levels. The highest level (shown in Figure 75) coincides with the aggregation level at which the WfMC reference architecture is defined (Figure 104). The second level details the main modules of the first level - the details of the context of the process engine are shown in Figure 76. The third level details the internals of the main modules at the second level.

As an example of the third level, we show the internals of the process engine in Figure 105. This architecture shows how a module of a BPMS is composed of sub-modules (in the terminology of the aggregation levels of Figure 22). In the architecture, we see how business process events are processed by sub-modules from top to bottom in the middle column of the architecture:

- first, events are received and standardized by the *event receptor sub-module*; events can arrive from workflow client modules via the *WFC Interface* or from the *clock sub-module*;

- then, events are analyzed by the *event analyzer* sub-module for processing, using the process definition data (describing what needs to be done in a process) and the process execution data (describing what already has been done);

- next, event are transformed into actions (things to do next in the business process) by the *action synthesizer* sub-module;

- finally, actions are executed by the *action executor* sub-module by sending them to other modules through their respective interfaces.

This processing structure follows the pipe-and-filter architecture pattern (see the pattern taxonomy in Figure 67). Further details on the Mercurius architecture can be found in [Gre98].

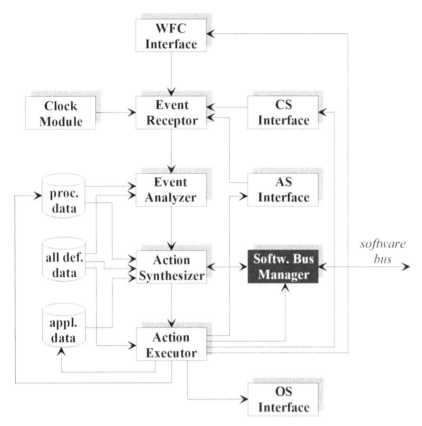

Figure 105: model at the third aggregation level of the Mercurius reference architecture

The aggregation level of Figure 105 is important to understand how a business process management system (BPMS) works 'on the inside' and hence what to expect from a detailed functionality point of view in process management. To design a process-driven corporate information system, however, this level is too detailed. Therefore, we return to a higher level of aggregation in the next subsection to discuss an application case.

7.2.3 Concrete architecture

We see a concrete BPMS application architecture in Figure 106, which is based on the WfMC reference architecture discussed above and in Section 4.3.2. We have included the WfMC interface numbering in the figure for easy reference. The concrete architecture is that of the BPM architecture of an insurance firm. The information systems of the insurance firm itself are modeled within the large, dashed box; the system outside the box is that of an insurance claim expertise bureau that the firm works with.

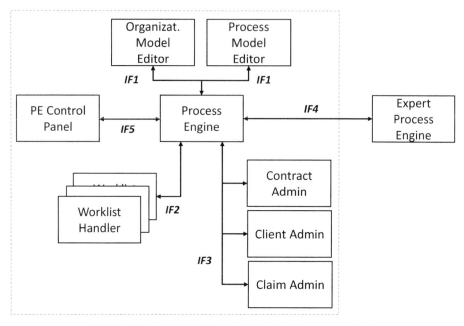

Figure 106: concrete BPM architecture (insurance firm)

At the center of the architecture, we see a single process engine. One engine will do in this case, as it is a relatively small firm. The engine interfaces with the worklist handlers through IF2 to drive manual tasks in the operational processes of the firm (the firm has about 50 employees using worklist handlers). The engine interfaces with the three main administrative application systems of the firm (contract, client and claim administration systems[41]) through IF3 to control automated tasks.

To define business processes, an organization model editor is used to specify the roles and actors, and a process model editor to specify the tasks and processes. A process engine control panel is used to manage the operation of the process engine. For business processes in which an expert claim assessment is required, the process engine of the firm connects to an external process engine that controls the expert claim assessment tasks, which are performed by employees of the insurance claim expertise bureau. This means that IF4 is used for business process outsourcing in this case.

---

[41] Note that these application systems (as their name suggests) are not part of the infrastructure layer of the architecture, but of the application layer (see Figure 91). The systems are shown in Figure 106 'next to' systems in the infrastructure layer to retain the architecture layout of the WfMC reference architecture (see Figure 104) for easy comparison.

7.3 Application system architecture

In this section, we discuss an example application system architecture. Where there are reference architectures for systems that support specific tasks that recur across organization types (like we have seen for data warehousing and business process management in the preceding sections of this chapter), there are often no reference architectures for systems that are specific to an organization type (or a class of organizations). Hence, we skip the treatment of a reference architecture here and immediately discuss a concrete architecture below. After we have discussed the architecture, we pay explicit attention to interoperability patterns between modules in this architecture.

7.3.1 Architecture structure

For our example, we return to the Trans-Oceanic Airways (TOA) airline company that we have already seen in Section 7.1.2 (and before). Where we have concentrated on the support for their decision making there, we concentrate on the support for their primary process here.

In Figure 107, we see the (heavily simplified) architecture of their information system landscape for their primary processes, their Operations Management Information System (we have seen this also as an example in Chapter 3 to illustrate the use of aggregation levels). The term 'landscape' refers to a collection of information systems in this context.

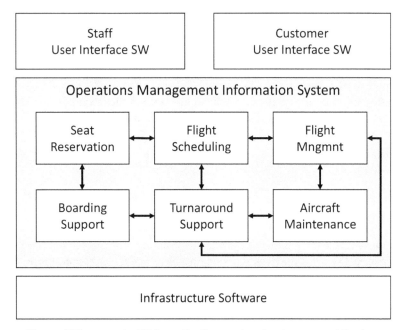

Figure 107: example TOA application system landscape architecture

In the figure, we see six main information systems with their user interface software 'on top' and their infrastructure software 'below' (in a layered architecture style as we have seen in Section 6.1). The six main information systems are the following:

Seat Reservation is used to reserve seats on flights. It is used both by TOA staff and by customers through a Web-based reservation system (hence, there are two kinds of user interface systems in the top layer of the architecture).

Boarding Support is used by TOA and airport staff when a flight is actually boarded. The system administers checked-in luggage and boarded passengers.

Turnaround Support is used by TOA and airport staff to prepare an aircraft for its next flight ('turning an airplane around' is the air travel domain term for this), including cleaning, refueling, and loading of food and beverages.

Aircraft Maintenance is used by TOA staff and specialized maintenance companies to support the maintenance of aircraft - both scheduled and emergency maintenance.

Flight Management is used by TOA staff to execute the company's flight schedules, e.g., the assign specific aircraft and crews to specific routes, dates and time slots.

Flight Scheduling is used by TOA staff to create new flight schedules on a periodic basis (it uses the Global Flight Planning Direct Query interface to the TOA data warehouse that we have seen in Figure 103).

The systems are connected by interfaces as shown in the architecture to exchange information. For example, Boarding Support interfaces with Seat Reservation to obtain the list of passengers who have tickets for a specific flight and hence will board a specific flight. To completely design and specify an application architecture, it is important to understand these interfaces. This goes both for understanding what data is exchanged via an interface and for how this data is exchanged. We discuss the nature of these interfaces in the next subsection below.

7.3.2 Interoperability patterns in the application architecture

In Section 4.2.3, we have discussed a simple catalog for interoperability patterns that describe the way information system components cooperate. Each pattern describes a way to exchange data with specific characteristics. We apply this catalog to the TOA architecture here to analyze the data flows in the architecture of Figure 107. For reasons of brevity, we choose two interfaces to analyze and leave the other interfaces for the reader to explore.

156

The first interface we analyze is the one that we have mentioned above: the one between the Seat Reservation and Boarding Support modules. The collaboration of these two information system modules is asynchronous: seats can be reserved during a long period before a flight and boarding support takes place only directly before the flight. This requires an asynchronous coupling, so we have a File Transfer or a Shared Database pattern (see Table 1 in Section 4.2.3). Next, we observe that the activities of the two systems can overlap in time (passengers may reserve a last-minute seat while boarding has commenced) and communication can be bi-directional (in the boarding process, corrections may have to be made to seat reservations). Hence, it is more practical to have a shared administration of seat reservations between the two systems than to exchange lists between them. The conclusion is that a Shared Database pattern is to be preferred here, as illustrated in Figure 108. The shared database holds the details of both seat reservations and the status of the boarding process (i.e., the indication of which seats have actually been filled by boarded passengers).

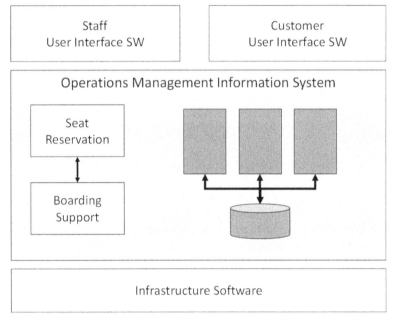

Figure 108: example interoperability pattern in TOA application architecture

Our second example interface is that between Flight Scheduling and Turnaround support. Here we see that the activities by Turnaround Support are based on flight schedules constructed by Flight scheduling on a periodic basis. This is an asynchronous and uni-directional exchange of data, with little interaction. Hence, after consulting Table 1 in Section 4.2.3, we determine that it can be implemented with a File Transfer pattern (shown on the left in Figure 109). But in case of emergencies that occur during turnaround (for example, an aircraft may appear to have technical problems), ad-hoc changes with a high time pressure must be made to flight schedules (for example, to modify a schedule or

157

to fly in a replacement aircraft). For this exception handling, Turnaround Support and Flight Scheduling need to be in synchronous, bi-directional contact. Here, we can choose either a Direct Invocation or a Shared Bus pattern. As TOA does not yet employ a shared bus and the interface at hand does not justify installing one, the Direct Invocation pattern is chosen, as illustrated on the right in Figure 109.

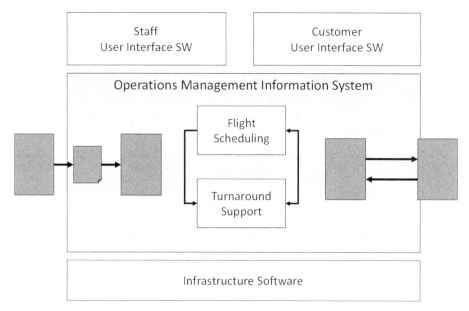

Figure 109: example interoperability patterns in TOA application architecture

This second example shows that detailed data flow analysis of an application architecture can reveal that one interface at an aggregated level actually consists of multiple interfaces at a more detailed level (going down the aggregation dimension as discussed in Section 3.3).

When we apply our above two analyses to the architecture shown in Figure 107, we obtain the refined architecture shown in Figure 110. After analyzing and specifying the other interfaces, the architecture can be further refined. Note that even for this simple architecture, this means analyzing six more interfaces. Being sloppy in the architecture design process here may lead to problems later in system realization. For example, if we would have skipped our first analysis above, we might have forgotten to include database management functionality in the system specification.

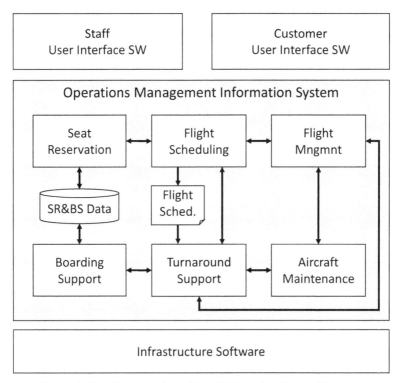

Figure 110: refined version of the TOA application architecture

7.3.3 Application architectures in enterprise architecting

In Section 6.2.3, we have introduced an architecture structure for the application layer of an enterprise-level system architecture (see Figure 95). This enterprise-level architecture shows how all application system architectures are related to each other. Consequently, to position an application architecture (like the one in Figure 107) in its enterprise-level context, we can 'insert' the application system architecture into the enterprise-level architecture. In doing so, we 'nest' two levels along the aggregation dimension of architecture.

Taking the example of Figure 107, we have an application architecture that supports part of the *operations* function of Porter's framework - as discussed in Section 6.2.3. Hence, this example architecture is part of the *operations* column of the enterprise-level architecture (assuming there is more support for the operations function - otherwise the example architecture coincides with the *operations* column). We have already shown this in an abstract way in the architecture of Figure 97. Now, we can relate the complete application system architecture (including its interfaces) to the enterprise architecture. We have illustrated this relation in Figure 111. Note that the user interface software level and infrastructure software level of Figure 107 are mapped to the corresponding levels of Figure 111 to allow reuse of functionality across application systems in different columns.

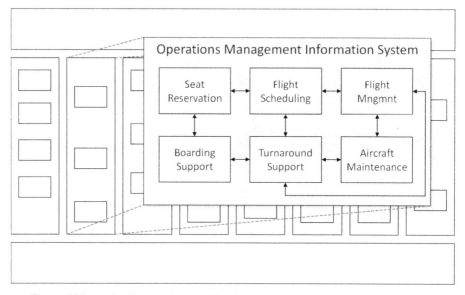

Figure 111: application system architecture in the context of enterprise system architecture

We have to note here that the above example is highly simplified, and reality is typically much more complex for several reasons:

- As already stated, the operations support column probably contains more information system components (like for example a staff planning system to organize the staffing of flights) and hence is more complex.

- Obviously, there are seven more columns to elaborate – each with its own complexity.

- Further, we have only shown interfaces between components within a column. But some components typically also have to communicate with components in other columns. For example, there may be communication between the system for seat reservations in the operations column and the system for online advertising in the marketing and sales column: flights that have many empty seats may require additional advertising.

Consequently, enterprise information architectures can easily contain hundreds of individual information system components, sometimes even several thousands of components for large enterprises. If such an architecture is not managed well, it may end up in utter chaos. This chaos is illustrated in Figure 112 for a small set of application information system – try and imagine this situation with hundreds of components.

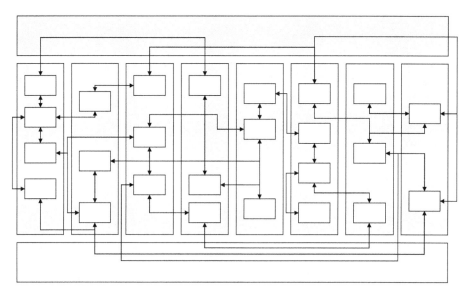

Figure 112: illustration of chaotic enterprise system architecture (to avoid!)

To avoid such a chaotic enterprise system architecture, a strict modularization at all architecture aggregation levels is essential. One way to achieve this is to try and keep the interfaces between columns as 'concentrated' as possible, i.e., have not all component systems communicate with each other across columns. The strict use of interoperability patterns (as we have illustrated in the previous subsection) also helps – the use of a bus or shared databases can reduce the required number of interfaces. And of course, (re)designing a system in a top-down way, navigating carefully along the dimensions of the architecture cube that we have seen in Section 3.6, typically helps a lot.

In the end, a well-designed corporate architecture leads to an effective and efficient use of digital technologies in an organization. We discuss these technologies in the next chapter.

8 TECHNOLOGIES FOR ARCHITECTURE EMBODIMENT

In this chapter, we focus our attention on information technologies for realizing systems that are described by architectures, i.e., on the topic of architecture embodiment. The goal of this chapter is not to provide a complete and detailed technology catalog geared towards the IT specialist, but to provide an overview of important digital technologies with the information system architect in mind. Having knowledge of this overview, an architect has a basis to understand choices in embodiment. Also, he or she is better able to communicate with the diverse technology experts – remember the role of an architect as discussed in Section 2.6 and illustrated in Figure 9.

In this chapter, we discuss technologies for architecture embodiment in two classes of system technologies that coincide with the application and infrastructure layers discussed in Chapter 6 of this book. We end this chapter with a short explanation of the question where discussions (and decisions) about architecture embodiment belong in a complete architecture development path.

In the next chapter, we pay attention to middleware technologies, as these are important as a 'digital glue' to connect software modules within and between the application and infrastructure layers, i.e., to integrate the application of technologies that we discuss in this chapter.

8.1 Application system technologies

When deciding about technologies for realizing application systems, an important decision is often whether to use a 'make' approach (i.e., have a dedicated solution constructed for a specific situation) or a 'buy' approach (i.e., select a standard system that best fits a specific situation). We discuss both alternatives in the two subsections below.

Before we discuss the alternatives, we have to remark that in modern times, typically the 'buy' approach is the preferred choice. Firstly, information systems have become so complex, that a 'make' approach for one application is often simply infeasible from a financial (or effort) perspective. Buying standard solutions is usually cheaper than building them to custom specifications [Gre11]. Secondly, interoperability beyond the boundaries of single firms has become increasingly important (e.g., for networked e-business [Gre16]), making the use of standardized systems more attractive.

8.1.1 Make-oriented technologies

In the 'make' approach, an application system is completely realized in a tailor-made fashion to comply with the requirements of a specific application scenario (architecture and further functional and non-functional specifications). Obviously, for complex application systems, the make approach can cause high costs (and long realization times).

Make-oriented technologies typically rely on programming environments to realize software. In the old days[42], COBOL environments [Wi24k] would be used for example for the realization of administrative information systems. These systems would often have a monolithic architecture style (see Section 4.1) and hence a closed character. Nowadays, we find more advanced object-oriented environments based on languages like Java. These can be used to embody *distributed object architectures* (DOA), which have an object-oriented architecture style (see Section 4.1).

Programming (or software engineering) environments can offer advanced libraries that contain software modules for specific purposes, thereby decreasing the need to develop everything from scratch. If these modules get very large and are acquired commercially, they start to resemble the situation of buy-oriented technology.

An alternative to using programming environments is using generator environments, where software code is generated based on detailed specifications. These detailed specifications, however, can be considered

---

[42] Even though some technologies may be (very) old, we still find legacy systems around in business practice that were built with these old technologies. Often, maintenance of these systems has become a major problem for the organizations using them.

programming code on a higher level of abstraction, for example in a domain-specific language [Fow10].

8.1.2 Buy-oriented technologies

In the 'buy' approach, an architecture module is embodied by buying an existing system that best meets the requirements of a specific application scenario. Such a bought system is often referred to as a 'common off the shelve' (COTS) solution. Advanced COTS systems are parameterizable such that their functionality can be tuned towards a specific application context. Obviously, a COTS system will not always meet the application requirements perfectly. Typically, however, COTS solutions can be realized much faster and cheaper than tailor-made solutions.

In the buy approach, one can buy individual systems or complete application landscapes. Individual systems focus on the support of a single business function or a set of closely related business functions. Obviously, interoperability of individual systems is a major requirement to arrive at well-connected enterprise solutions. Adherence to middleware standards (as discussed in the next chapter of this book) is an important aspect in this context.

Application landscapes focus on the support of a large part of the business functions of an organization. Enterprise resource planning (ERP) systems are an example of the latter category, providing support for a spectrum of business functions. In the case of complex application landscapes, parameterizing these for a specific context can be a major effort (that sometimes resembles a large programming effort).

8.2 Infrastructure system technologies

Infrastructure system technologies are hardly ever specific to an application context – certainly not in a business context[43]. This means that infrastructure systems should hardly ever (or never at all) be of the 'make' type – typically it is wise to just buy them.

In this section, we discuss two classes of common infrastructure system technologies: database management technology and business process management technology (also known as workflow management technology). Of

---

[43] In some high-tech application domains (take for example space exploration), infrastructure systems may have to comply with such specific requirements that they have to be tailor-made. In a business context, this is hardly ever the case – even though some business problem owners may disagree with this. The latter may be a consequence of the *not-invented-here syndrome*: the (typically wrong) idea that an application context is so special, that everything has to be reinvented for this context.

course, there are more classes of infrastructure system technologies, but it goes beyond the scope of this book to discuss them all.

8.2.1 Database management technology

Database management technology is infrastructure system technology used to manage large sets of (business) data. The technology typically is available as a COTS solution in the form of a database management system (DBMS). Database management systems have been around since the 60's of the 20th century. Consequently, database management technology is one of the most mature technology classes in infrastructure technologies.

Below, we first discuss the internal architecture of database management systems. Then, we discuss the various classes of these systems.

DBMS architecture

To provide a 'peek under the hood' of database systems, we briefly describe their internal architecture below. Understanding of this technology is not essential for the deployment of database systems in application contexts, but helps in understanding their functionality and inherent complexity – and hence also in communicating with database technology experts.

An abstract internal architecture of a typical database management system is shown in Figure 113. The architecture contains the following modules:

- The *application interface* module provides the interface to application modules, i.e., software modules in the application layer of an IS or CIS architecture. Through the application interface, application modules can pass their commands to the DBMS – for example to store or to retrieve specified data.

- The *query translation* module translates commands from external, application-oriented formats to the internal, processing-oriented format. The availability of this module can allow for multiple application-oriented command languages to cater for different uses of the DBMS.

- The *query optimization module* transforms a command such that it can be efficiently processed by the underlying layers – this relieves the applications from the burden to be aware of the internal processing mechanisms of the DBMS.

- The *query execution module* oversees the execution of commands. It communicates with the transaction management module to obtain access to data in the context of multiple concurrent applications using the database.

- The actual execution of commands (or parts thereof), i.e. the low-level operations against the databases managed by the DBMS, is performed by the *data management module*.

- The *transaction management module* orchestrates the concurrent execution of multiple commands from various applications and/or users. Note that an enterprise DBMS can serve many applications/users at the same time – this can easily be in the order of thousands. This module ensures that all commands are executed in a *serializable* way, i.e., in a way that is in effect equivalent to a serial execution (i.e., without concurrency). This avoids unwanted effects of multiple applications/users changing the same data items concurrently. To achieve a correct serializable execution, application commands are grouped into transactions (which explains the name of the module).

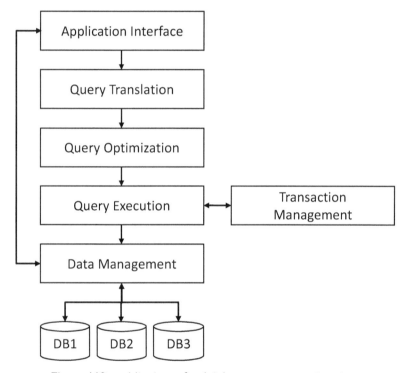

Figure 113: architecture of a database management system

Often, enterprise DBMSs have the form of a client/server system. This means that the application-oriented part (the client side) is technically decoupled from the data processing-oriented part (the server side). This way, the client side can be technically coupled to an application, thereby obtaining possibilities for efficiency gains and load balancing. An example client/server configuration is shown in Figure 114. Note that it is possible to have the boundary between clients and server also at other levels in the architecture. For example, if different clients use different query languages, dedicated query translation modules per client may replace the server-side query translation module.

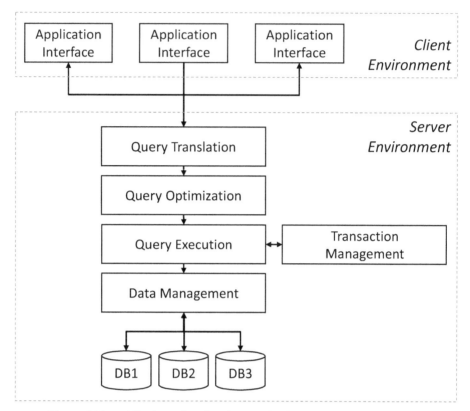

Figure 114: architecture of a client/server database management system

DBMS classes

From a functionality point of view, there are several classes of database management systems, which we can divide between legacy types and contemporary types.

Legacy DBMS types are types that have been introduced in the past but are not considered contemporary technology anymore. They can still be found in practice, however, as they may be woven such into a system landscape that it is very hard to replace them with more modern systems (creating a legacy problem). Obviously, this is not good architecture practice, but a result of poor practice in the past. Legacy DBMS types are:

- The network database management system is based on data organized as networks of pointers. CODASYL created a well-known standard for this class of DBMSs [Wi24n], which is generally considered old-fashioned nowadays.

- The hierarchical database management system is based on data organized in tree-like structures.

- The functional database management system relies on the notion of functions (tables of mappings between values) to organize data.

Contemporary DBMS types are considered contemporary technology. We can distinguish several classes:

- By far the most common type of contemporary DBMS is the *relational database management system* (RDBMS), which supports the well-known relational data model and the SQL language for database querying and manipulation. Most modern-day business applications rely on a RDBMS for their data management needs.

- A *multi-media database management system* (MMDBMS) is a DBMS that is geared towards the storage of multi-media information (such as sound or video). A MMDBMS can be an extension of a RDBMS.

- An *object-oriented database management system* (OODBMS) is a DBMS supports an object-oriented data model. An OODBMS is often designed to be integrated into an object-oriented software environment. The OODBMS class can for example be found in engineering application contexts (e.g., as support for CAD/CAM applications) – it is not popular in typical business application contexts.

- A *multi-dimensional database management system* is a system that is designed to work with a multi-dimensional data model. It is typically applied in complex data analysis (or data mining) environments for online analytical processing (OLAP) applications [Tho02], for example in business intelligence contexts coupled to data warehouses (as discussed in Section 7.1 of this book).

- A *NoSQL database management system* [Wi24e] is an extension of the class RDBMS that can also handle data and queries that do not conform to the relational data structure (hence the name *Not only SQL*).

A modern concept is that of 'data fabric'. This concept refers to a data management environment (as part of the infrastructure layer of an information system landscape) that offers various types of data management (like relational database management for business applications, NoSQL-style data management for document repositories, and OLAP-style data management for business intelligence).

8.2.2 Business process management technology

Business process management technology (also referred to as workflow management technology) is information technology to manage the design and execution of complex, well-specified business processes that are typically performed by many actors in large organizations. Comparable to DBMSs for data management, the technology is available in COTS form as business process management systems (BPMSs) or workflow management systems (WFMSs).

BPMSs have been around as COTS solutions from around the middle of the 1990s. They do not yet have the maturity of DBMSs, however, which shows for example in a lesser degree of standardization. An important, be it high-level, step in standardization was the establishment of the WfMC reference architecture [Hol95], which we have discussed in Section 4.3 and Section 7.2. Another important step in the standardization of business process management technology was the establishment of the BPMN language [Fre19] to specify business processes. BPMS systems have not yet been accepted to the same degree by business practice as DBMS systems.

Business process management technology does not always have the exact form as described before. We can observe several different forms:

- A variation on a business process management system is a (dynamic) *case management system* [Kar24]. Such a system works comparably, but instead of a well-defined process that prescribes an order of working, it uses a loosely defined process specification that is used to prevent incorrect ways of process execution.

- We also find business process management technology embedded into other technology, such as enterprise resource planning (ERP) technology, or even specific application system technology. Usually, this is not preferable, as it hampers a proper layering in the architecture and hence decreases the modifiability of it (see also the discussion in Section 6.1.2).

8.3 The place of embodiment discussions

Discussions (and hence decisions) about architecture embodiment are about the choice and positioning of specific information technology for realizing information systems that are described by architectures. The place of these discussions in an architecture development path can be discussed in the context of the architecture development cube that we have discussed in Section 3.6.

In Figure 115, we have marked the typical position of these embodiment discussions in the architecture cube by coloring the corresponding eight cells of the cube dark (to make things better visible, we have made cells in the front of the cube transparent).

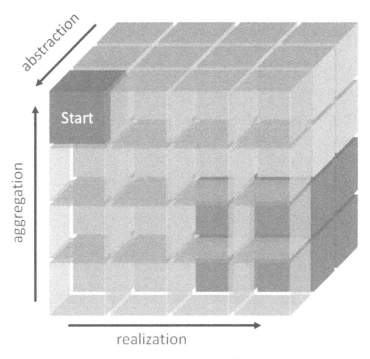

Figure 115: place of embodiment in the IS development cube

As shown in Figure 115, embodiment choices typically play a role in the second half of the realization dimension, as specific technology choices are not often a requirement to start an architecture design path with.

Embodiment aspects become important when decisions become more concrete, so not at the highest level of abstraction. Consequently, the marked cells in the figure are in the lower values of the abstraction dimension.

Finally, specific technologies are typically not yet visible at high levels of aggregation. At high levels of aggregation, they are typically encapsulated into large modules hiding the technology. Consequently, we have marked the cells in the figure in the lower half of the aggregation dimension.

Note that the dark sub-cube representing the place of the embodiment choices in Figure 115 is an illustration only – the exact location depends on the nature of a development project and of course on the precise choice of the (number of) values per dimension – but typically it will be in a 'bottom-back-right' part of the cube. In most circumstances, choices of specific technologies should follow high-level business choices, not the other way around.

9
MIDDLEWARE
TECHNOLOGIES

After having discussed database management and business process management technologies as infrastructure technologies in the preceding chapter, we now turn our attention to middleware technologies as part of infrastructures. Middleware technologies provide the 'glue' in most modern-day enterprise business information system landscapes: they allow individual systems to communicate with each other in a structured but flexible way.

For many, middleware technologies are much harder to understand than the database management and process management classes of technology, because middleware is much more 'invisible', i.e., it provides functionality that cannot so easily be pointed at as the other two technologies for the non-expert. For an information system architect, understanding the basics of middleware is essential, however.

Below, we start with explaining why this 'invisible' class of technology is actually so important for complex information systems. In Section 9.2, we explain what middleware is and which classes of middleware we can distinguish. Each of these five classes is next treated in some detail. We end this chapter in Section 9.8 with a short discussion on the introduction of middleware into existing system landscapes (i.e., how to deal with middleware in legacy situations).

9.1 The need for middleware

Corporate information systems are getting more and more complex and more and more connected. The increasing complexity is caused by the fact that more and more business functions are supported by automated systems and that the complexity of the individual functions increases as well. The increasing connectivity is caused by the fact that business functions need to be tightly integrated into efficient business processes[44], thus requiring automated connections between the systems supporting these functions. As we have seen in Chapter 7 of this book, we can thus get to complex connectivity situations as illustrated in Figure 116 (repeated from that chapter). As we have already discussed, this figure is a huge simplification of many situations in practice where we may have hundreds or sometimes even thousands of interconnected systems. Whenever a new system is added, things get more complex. But also when the functionality of an existing component is extended, it may need more interfaces to other systems – and things get more complex with respect to the communication topology.

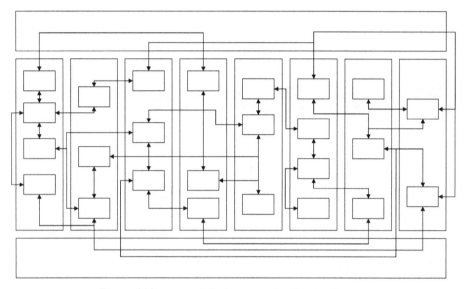

Figure 116: connectivity in an application landscape

9.1.1 Connecting application systems

Because of the increasing complexity and connectivity, we can get into the situation of a 'connection explosion' between application systems. To get an idea of the severity of this, connectivity between a simple configuration of four application systems is schematically illustrated in Figure 117. Here we see that a topology with four application systems can lead to six bi-directional interfaces (or twelve uni-directional interfaces).

---

[44] As stated in a catalog of business architecture principles, processes should be straight through [Gre11].

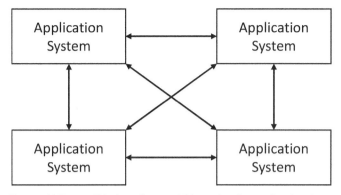

Figure 117: possible interfaces within a simple application layer

If all systems are interconnected (which is the worst-case scenario), the number of connections (interfaces) is in the order of the square of the number of systems. More precisely, if the number of application systems is as, the maximum number of bi-directional connections c_{max} is given by the simple formula:

$$c_{max} = \frac{as(as - 1)}{2}$$

Obviously, the number of connections can get truly huge in case of typical application landscapes in large organizations that consist of hundreds or even thousands of individual systems. Of course, not all systems are typically connected to all other systems, but even if connectivity is far less, very complex 'spaghetti-like' topologies can emerge – and every change in functionality may change the topology, making it hard to keep a consistent overview.

The connection explosion problem can be addressed by not connecting all systems on a pair-by-pair basis, but by connecting them all individually to a common interconnect, which routes the communication between the systems. To use a very simple analogy, this can be compared to using a telephone exchange system instead of connecting all telephones directly to each other. In this way, the number of connections increases only linearly with the number of systems:

$$c_{max} = as$$

Such a common interconnect is called middleware, as illustrated in Figure 118. Note that conceptually, the use of middleware is very similar to using the bus architecture pattern, as discussed in Section 4.2.

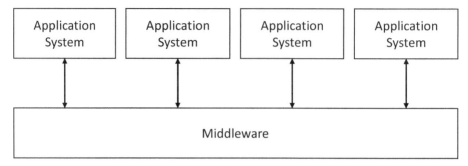

Figure 118: application layer organized with middleware

9.1.2 Connecting application and infrastructure systems

When we look at the connections between application layer systems and infrastructure layer systems, we see a similar problem, as illustrated in Figure 119. As the functionality of application system systems increases, these systems require more and more interfaces to infrastructure layer systems.

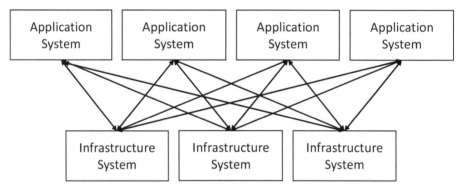

Figure 119: possible interfaces between application layer and infrastructure layer

The maximum number of connections in a topology like shown in Figure 119 is (with *as* for the number of application systems, and *is* for the number of infrastructure systems):

$$c_{max} = as \times is$$

This problem can be solved with a common interconnect (again middleware) as well, as illustrated in Figure 120. Here, the middleware forms an interface layer between application layer systems and infrastructure layer systems.

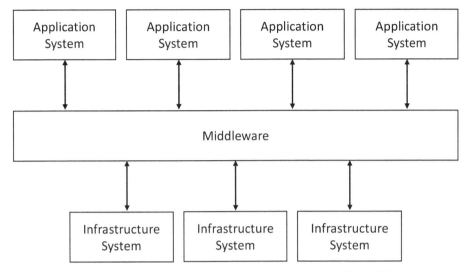

Figure 120: application and infrastructure layer connected by middleware

Again, the use of middleware reduces the maximum number of required interfaces to a linear formula:

$$c_{max} = as + is$$

After we have seen why middleware is required in complex system landscapes from a communication topology perspective, we turn to the nature of middleware in the next section (where we also explain that there are even more reasons to use middleware).

9.2 What is middleware?

Middleware is software that is 'in the middle' between other software components (or systems). As we have seen in the previous section, it facilitates the 'orderly' connection of large sets of components without getting confronted with an 'interface explosion': it helps reducing the number of interfaces between systems from one governed by a quadratic formula to one governed by a linear formula.

A bit more technically put, middleware is software designed to effectively and efficiently facilitate the interconnection of a large set of software components in a complex environment. The 'effectively and efficiently' means that a middleware solution will automatically address a number of 'problematic' characteristics of a set of software components, such that the designers (or deployers) of these components do not need to bother about this. In this way, the use of middleware brings more benefits than only topology simplification as discussed in the previous section.

These problematic characteristics addressed can be any the following:

- Heterogeneity of implementation language: the middleware resolves interconnection problems that are a result of different implementation languages used for software components.

- Heterogeneity of deployment platform: the middleware resolves interconnection problems that are a result of different platforms (such as operation systems) used for various components.

- Heterogeneity of technical interconnection: the middleware resolves interconnection problems caused by different technical interconnections (such as wired or wireless networks) between components.

- Distribution of the set of modules: the middleware will allow the software designer to view all software modules as centralized (physically located at the same site), despite the fact that they may be physically distributed across a complex computer network (even across the entire Internet).

Summarizing, we can say the following: the use of middleware takes a lot of the burden of complexity from the shoulders of a software designer in a complex, distributed environment. Obviously, nothing comes for free: the middleware itself is additional software, and usually not of a trivial complexity (but typically available as a COTS component).

As can be concluded from the above, middleware plays an important role in the technical embodiment of complex architectures. This means that in the realization dimension of architectures (as discussed in Section 3.5), middleware comes into play in the IT-oriented part of this dimension. Its role is also important in concrete, detailed architectures. As such, the place of middleware in the architecture modeling cube is comparable to that of other embodiment technologies, as discussed in Section 8.3 and illustrated in Figure 115.

In general, we can distinguish between multiple classes of middleware depending on the mechanisms used by the middleware and the interconnection problems it focuses on:

- Database-oriented middleware
- Function-oriented middleware
- Message-oriented middleware
- Object-oriented middleware
- Service-oriented middleware

We discuss these five classes in some detail in the five sections that follow.

9.3 Database-oriented middleware

Database-oriented middleware is interconnectivity software that supports interfacing between application programs in the application layer on the one hand and database management systems in the infrastructure layer on the other hand.

Database-oriented middleware can provide a number of functionalities:

- Unifying the technical interface to a heterogeneous set of database management systems, i.e., enabling all systems to be contacted in the same way.

- Unifying the language interface to a heterogeneous set of database management systems, i.e., offering one single database management command language to applications despite the fact that the database management systems themselves use different languages.

- Managing load balancing in a database environment with replicated server functionality (having multiple database servers that can perform the same tasks), i.e., routing application requests such that throughput and response times are optimized.

- Managing application transactions that span multiple database systems, i.e., making sure that changes to multiple autonomous database systems can be guaranteed to remain consistent from an application point of view, even when system failures occur (referred to as consistency control or integrity control).

The use of database-oriented middleware is typically based on a layered architecture style (see Section 4.1.3), following the application versus infrastructure separation as discussed in Section 6.1. The resulting architecture structure is illustrated in Figure 121 – note the similarity in client/server structure with Figure 114.

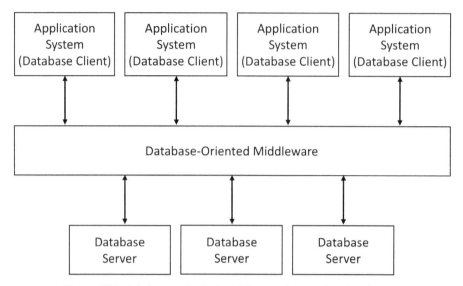

Figure 121: database-oriented middleware in a system landscape

9.4 Function-oriented middleware

Function-oriented middleware is the oldest class of middleware that targets inter-application system communication. It was designed to facilitate interoperability between large software modules such as programs. It does so by supporting program-to-program function invocation, for example by remote procedure call (RPC) mechanisms.

Using an RPC mechanism, one program can synchronously invoke a function (called a *procedure* in the RPC context) that is implemented in another program that may be running on a different platform (see the illustration in Figure 122). Synchronous invocation means that the invoking program waits for the answer of the invoked program. This implies that the progress of the invoker program depends on the progress of the invoked program.

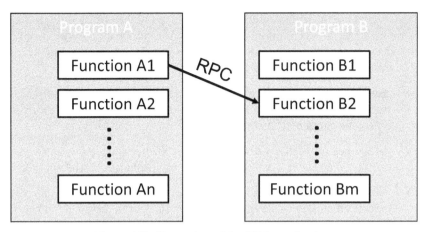

Figure 122: illustration of the RPC mechanism

This traditional style of function-oriented middleware targeting large software modules can be seen as based on a combination of the monolithic style and either the columned or the layered style (see Section 4.1). It uses programs as monoliths that invoke remote functions in other monoliths. In the columned approach, the communication uses peer-to-peer invocation (for example, between application programs). In the layered approach, the communication uses client/server invocation (for example, between an application program and a database management program).

9.5 Message-oriented middleware

Message-oriented middleware is program-to-program (or information system to information system) communication middleware that is based on the exchange of messages. In many ways, the concept is comparable to people-to-people communication that relies on the exchange of emails. In essence, it has the same general aim as function-oriented middleware (as discussed in Section 9.4), but instead of synchronous procedure invocation it uses asynchronous message passing. This means that if one component needs an answer from another component, a pair of messages is needed: one in one direction to send a request, one in the other direction to deliver the answer.

The principle of asynchronous message passing offers the possibilities for very loosely coupled systems: one program in principle only needs the address of another program to be able to communicate (and hence collaborate) with it – again like in the email paradigm. Loose coupling allows for dynamic system landscapes. The complexity of the message-oriented paradigm, however, comes with automatically understanding exchanged messages, i.e., with syntax and semantics of messages.

Typically, message-oriented middleware offers a number of quality guarantees to make sure that message processing can be fully automatically executed by a so-called message broker, i.e., does not have to rely on human interaction to resolve irregular situations. Such qualities are:

- Every sent message is guaranteed to be delivered exactly once, i.e., messages are not lost nor replicated by the middleware (even in the case of system malfunctions).

- Messages are delivered to a recipient in the same order as they were sent by the sender, such that inter-system protocols can be adhered to.

- Messages are delivered within a certain timeframe, i.e., there is a specified quality of service (QoS) with respect to message transport.

The message-oriented middleware paradigm is not strongly based on a specific architecture style, but comes closest to the component-oriented style (see Section 4.1), as its allows software components to communicate without restrictions imposed by layers or columns.

9.6 Object-oriented middleware

Object-oriented middleware supports object-to-object method invocation in a system based on a distributed object architecture (DOA). This means that this class of middleware takes a component-oriented architecture style (see Section 4.1.5) as a starting point. The middleware software allows objects to easily communicate with each other despite differences between them with respect to implementation characteristics, underlying platform, technical or geographical location, and technical interconnection between their underlying platforms.

Standards for object-oriented middleware have been developed mainly in the 1990's. We discuss two standards in the subsections below: CORBA and DCOM.

9.6.1 CORBA

One of the best-known standards for object-oriented middleware is CORBA (Common Object Request Broker Architecture) [OM04], which is the middleware standard for the Object Management Architecture (OMA). CORBA is by now considered a technically slightly outdated standard (often replaced by service-oriented middleware like we discuss in Section 9.7). We discuss it in this book nevertheless because of its well-structured architecture. This architecture can be used to structure (or understand) the design of systems based on more contemporary middleware technology.

Object Management Architecture

We have already briefly discussed CORBA and OMA as reference architectures in Section 4.3.3. We show the basic OMA architecture again in Figure 123.

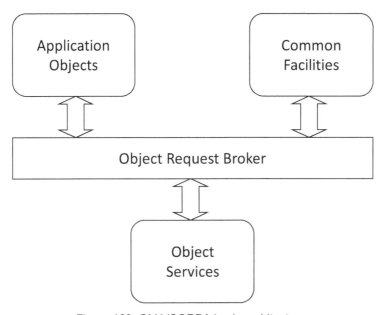

Figure 123: OMA/CORBA basic architecture.

The actual middleware in this architecture is the object request broker (ORB) (specified by the CORBA standard). The three sets of objects around it (*application objects*, *common facilities*, and *object services*) are not part of the middleware, as they do not provide interconnection functionality. These sets of objects help in grouping objects and making groups reusable across application scenarios such that information system realization efforts can be decreased. The *object services* contain reusable low-level functionality that is not specific to an application scenario. Examples of this functionality are object class and instance management and storage management. The *common facilities* contain reusable high-level functionality that is not specific to an application scenario. Examples of this functionality are user interface elements, and print and mail support. The *application objects* contain the functionality that is specific for an application. The idea is that in the development of a new application, the *application objects* are developed and objects in the other two sets are reused (i.e., typically bought in a standard package).

Communicating through a CORBA ORB

The way communication via CORBA-compliant middleware works is very basically shown in Figure 124. Here we see that one object (called the object client) needs to contact another object (called the object server) to access its functionality. Each of the two objects can be in any of the three object sets identified in OMA and shown in Figure 123.

183

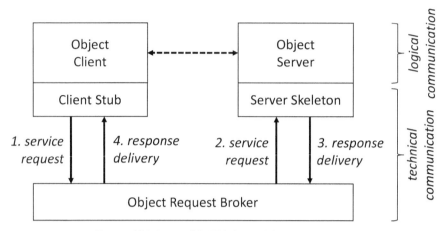

Figure 124: basic CORBA inter-object mechanism

The connection appears (at the application or logical level level) to be directly between the two objects, shown by the dashed arrow in Figure 124. The technical connection is made through the object request broker (ORB), however, as shown by the solid arrows in the figure. To realize this mechanism in an automated fashion, the object client is equipped with a so-called *client stub*, which intercepts inter-objects requests and routes these to the ORB. The ORB analyzes the request, locates the identified object server, and transfers and translates the request if necessary. The object server is equipped with a so-called *server skeleton*, which receives the request from the ORB and passes it to the object server like a direct request. The answer from object server to object client follows the reverse path. In this way, objects can communicate in a transparent way without being aware of location, technical context or technical implementation of each other - as all of this is resolved by the ORB. If the two objects are connected to different ORBs, these ORBs can connect via the Internet Inter-ORB Protocol (IIOP). Further details on the use of CORBA can be found in technical guides (for example in [Bol01]).

When we combine the OMA/CORBA architecture of Figure 123 with the communication mechanism of Figure 124, we get a situation where all communication between pairs of objects is routed through the ORB at the technical level, as illustrated in Figure 125. Note again that at the logical (application) level, objects appear to communicate with each other directly.

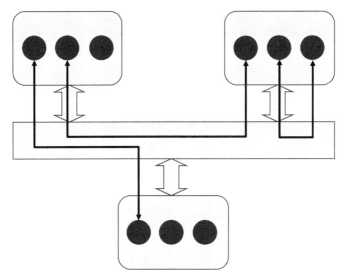

Figure 125: technical communication in OMA/CORBA

The Interface Definition Language

In the CORBA standard, interfaces of objects are specified using the Interface Definition Language (IDL). This language is used both for specifying object functionality and for implementing interoperability between objects. As such, IDL has a dual focus, as illustrated in Figure 126.

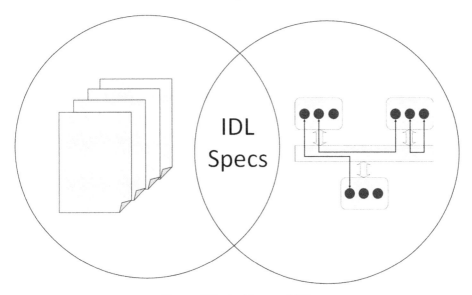

Figure 126: dual focus of IDL

Often, there is some confusion about the terminology around CORBA - reason to clarify this here (see also Figure 127). The CORBA specification is part of the OMA specification, which are both set as standards by the OMG (Object

185

Management Group), as illustrated in the left-hand side of Figure 127. A specific compliant ORB (Object Request Broker) is a piece of software (the actual middleware) that implements the CORBA specifications. A specific ORB (like ORBIX) is built by a specific software provider (like MF), as illustrated in the right-hand side of Figure 127. Summarizing, there is a 'world of standards' (in which specifications are predominant) and a 'world of systems' (in which software is predominant), as illustrated by the two columns in the figure.

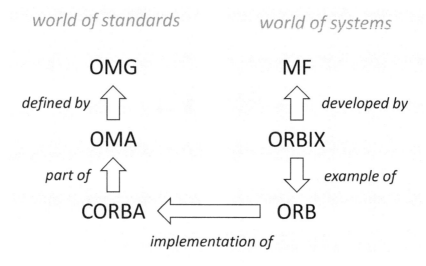

Figure 127: terminology around CORBA

9.6.2 DCOM

Another well-known standard is for object-oriented middleware is DCOM (Distributed Component Object Model), which was developed as proprietary technology by Microsoft[45]. Where CORBA is a 'de jure' standard (because it has been standardized by a standardization body), DCOM is a 'de facto' standard (because it is an inherent part of a very popular operating system: Microsoft Windows). DCOM was a major competitor to CORBA [Wi24l].

Details on the use of DCOM can be found in technical guides (for example [Tha99]).

---

[45] DCOM was originally called Network OLE, where OLE is short for Object Linking and Embedding.

9.7 Service-oriented middleware

Service-oriented middleware is in many ways comparable to object-oriented middleware but follows the more recent service-oriented paradigm instead of the older object-oriented paradigm. As we have seen in Section 4.1, both paradigms follow the component-oriented style: in object-oriented middleware, an object is a component; in service-oriented middleware, a service is a component. Like object-oriented middleware supports distributed method invocation for collaboration between objects, service-oriented middleware supports distributed service invocation for collaboration between services.

9.7.1 Web Service technology

Service-oriented middleware is technically often associated with the Web Service paradigm [New02, Alo04] (though in principle, it can also be realized in other ways). The Web Service paradigm is regarded as *the* standard paradigm for the realization of distributed information systems that use the Internet (and intranets) as the communication infrastructure.

Using the Web Service paradigm implies using the Web Service (WS) technology stack. This technology stack defines a number of related standard languages and protocols for communication and synchronization in a service-oriented context. Figure 128 shows a typical Web Services technology stack (but many other variations on this stack exist, depending on which standards are included).

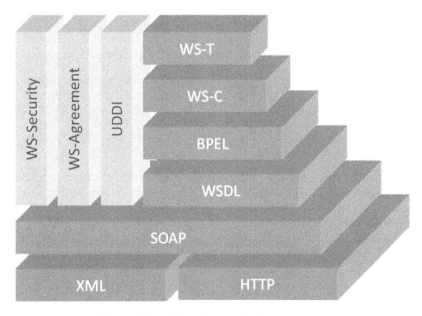

Figure 128: a Web Service technology stack

187

In the stack of Figure 128, we have elements that are shown horizontal and elements that are shown vertical. The ones shown vertical can be considered extensions of the more basic stack consisting of the horizontal elements. We describe the elements briefly below:

XML: The eXtensible Markup Language is a tag-based (hence *markup*) meta-language to define other languages (hence *extensible*) in the context of the Web.

HTTP: The HyperText Transfer Protocol is the basic protocol for transferring messages via the Web using URLs (Uniform Resource Locators).

SOAP: The Simple Object Access Protocol is a communication protocol allowing objects to access each other, using HTTP and XML as its underlying standards.

WSDL: The Web Service Definition Language is a language to describe the interface of Web Services, i.e., the way functionality of components can be accessed.

BPEL: The Business Process Execution Language is a language to specify business processes in terms of Web Services; as such, it can be seen as a language to specify the control flow of a business process in which the activities (steps) are specified as Web Services.

WS-C/WS-T: The WS Coordination and WS Transaction standards specify standards to coordinate the distributed execution of related Web Services, i.e., ensure that a set of Web Services has a consistent behavior.

UDDI: Universal Description, Discovery and Integration is a standard for platform-independent, Extensible Markup Language (XML)-based registries (brokers) by which businesses worldwide can list themselves on the Internet, and a mechanism to register and locate web service applications [Apt02].

WS-Agreement: WS-Agreement is a standard for specifying agreements (such as service level agreements) between parties collaborating through Web Services.

WS-Security: WS-Security is a standard for specifying security requirements to Web Service infrastructures.

As can be concluded from the above description of standards, the technology stack of Figure 128 is a heterogeneous stack, as it mixes standards for languages (which specify standards for *what* is exchanged in a Web Service context) and standards for protocols (which specify standards for *how* to exchange things in a Web Service context). It is important, however, not to mix up the respective functions of languages and protocols in designing a Web Service application context.

9.7.2 A simple Web Service application scenario

Service-oriented middleware is typically used for the realization of service-oriented software, which in turn can support service-oriented (or even service-dominant [Lüf12]) business. In this subsection, we briefly illustrate this in an abstract scenario.

A simple application scenario with some of the discussed Web Service standards is shown in Figure 129. Here we see four interacting Web Services SA, SB, SC and SD (belonging to three organizations, as indicated by the dotted boxes), and one Broker (typically operated by a fourth, independent party). The interface of each of the Web Services is specified in WSDL (as indicated for service SD). The internal control flow of composed services is specified in BPEL (as indicated for service SA). Coordination between the execution of services is specified in WS-C and WS-T (as indicated for services SB, SC and SD). Services register themselves with the Broker using the UDDI standard and find other services through the Broker using the UDDI standard. In the example, service SB registers itself with the Broker such that it can be found and invoked by other services. Service SA accesses the Broker to find service SB and this way can include the invocation of SB in its service composition.

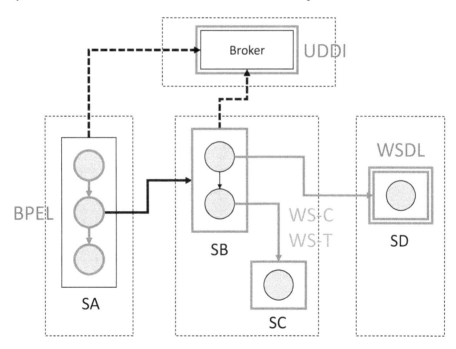

Figure 129: simple application scenario with Web Service standards

189

9.7.3 SOA and ESB

In this section so far, we have seen Web Service standards and their application. Just as in an any component-oriented architecture, having many interacting services (components) around can (and will, if not properly managed) cause a chaotic situation. As we have discussed in the beginning of this chapter, this calls for the use of structured middleware to organize the situation. Doing so, we arrive at a service-oriented architecture (SOA).

The most common form of service-oriented middleware for business applications is an Enterprise Service Bus (ESB), which is a communications broker that connects services in the context of a corporate information system.

We see an example of the use of an ESB in an architecture in Figure 130. Here, as the ESB connects a number of business services - all communication between the services is routed through the ESB. Note that this architecture is a technical realization (based on the ESB principle) of the abstract architecture of Organization B in Figure 60.

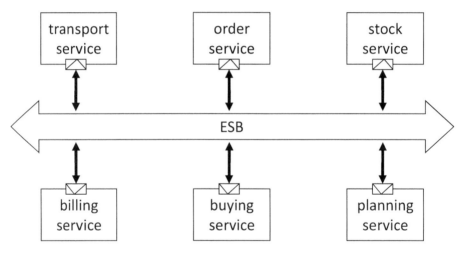

Figure 130: ESB in CIS

An ESB in its service-oriented context is in many ways comparable to an ORB in its object-oriented context (as discussed in Section 9.6).

9.8 Introducing middleware into an application landscape

Middleware is a pervasive technology class from an architectural point of view. It connects everything together, comparable to the artery system or the nervous system in the human body from a biological point of view. The choice of middleware influences many architectural decisions, both high-level (such as

190

the main architecture styles used) and low-level (such as the nature of interfaces between architectural components). This implies that dealing with middleware is a very important issue for the architect and very much depends on the starting situation: greenfield or legacy.

9.8.1 Greenfield versus legacy scenarios

When we have a greenfield starting point, the architecture of an organization is to be designed from scratch. This means that all important decisions can be taken more or less freely, for example those around middleware. Consequently, a homogeneous and consistent situation can be designed without pre-existing technical constraints. Unfortunately, greenfield situations are rare for the architect: they only exist when new organizations start up (and have a complex information system requirement from the very start) or when existing system landscapes have grown that incredibly bad that a complete and utter, big-bang replacement is the only option.

In a legacy situation, the situation is completely different: an application landscape is already in existence. Depending on the age (and technical innovation capabilities) of an organization, the landscape may already be old (which in IT terms typically means a few decades). Depending on the size of the organization, the landscape may be very complex (as we saw before, up to thousands of application and infrastructure systems). Middleware may be in place or not. And if it is in place, it may be old-fashioned, heterogeneous (as a result of non-harmonized system development in the past), or both. Here, the old and the new need to be integrated. As in the architecture of buildings (illustrated in Figure 131), this is usually not an easy task.

Figure 131: integrating the old and the new: the Royal Library in Copenhagen with the old wing to the far left and the new wing (called the Black Diamond) to the right (photo by author)

9.8.2 Evolution towards middleware

When one wants to introduce a uniform middleware solution into a legacy situation, this typically means a well-planned, gradual evolution path from the current CIS architecture to a future CIS architecture. Such a path may well take up to a decade to fully implement. The gradual evolution means that systems in the system landscape will be transformed on an individual basis from the old to the new situation. This implies that there will be a long period with middleware-compliant systems and non-middleware-compliant systems that live side-to-side.

To be able to roll out a middleware infrastructure as soon as possible and replace old infrastructures, it may be worthwhile to enable the non-middleware-compliant systems to operate in a middleware environment, even though their 'internals' were not designed for this. This can be accomplished by so-called 'wrapping' of systems: systems are encapsulated into a middleware-compliant software packaging (the 'wrapper') such that they appear middleware-compliant on the 'outside'. The wrapper has the duty to convert all communication between the system and its environment from the middleware standard to the internal mechanisms and the other way around.

Figure 132 shows a simple example of an application landscape in transition towards a middleware basis. Some systems are already middleware-compliant – they fit the modern architecture. Two legacy application systems have been wrapped with a middleware-compliant wrapper. This way, they can communicate with other MW-compliant systems using the middleware infrastructure system. One of the wrapped systems functions as an interface to the legacy systems that have not been wrapped: it is a 'bridge' between the modern part of the system landscape and the legacy part.

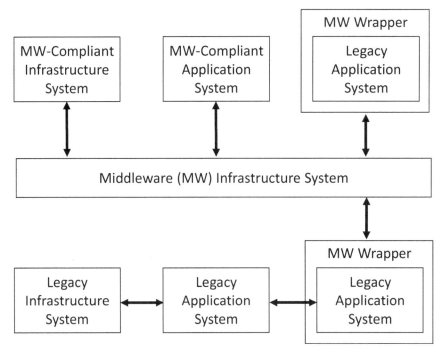

Figure 132: wrapping of legacy systems in a CORBA context

Usually, transition situations in practice are much more complex than shown in Figure 132. These situations are by definition a compromise and hence should not exist too long for several reasons. For example, two kinds of technology need to be maintained in parallel (with the associated costs), the used wrappers may be limited in functionality (with the associated limitations to business operations), and not all optimal connections between systems are operational.

10 ARCHITECTURE IN RETROSPECTIVE

In this short final chapter, we conclude this book by briefly looking in retrospect at the importance of the field of business information system architecture and the role of the architect in this field.

10.1 The importance of IS architecture

In all domains of industry and society, we see an ever-increasing complexity of information systems. More and more functions are being automated, leading to more and more information systems or information system modules. And these functions need to be interconnected, within the boundaries of organizations and across these. Take for example the banking industry, where an almost complete transition has been made from a heavily paper-based to an almost completely digital industry. Many other industries follow the same path. In society, for example, social media have quickly gained importance, leading to large volumes of digital interactions between humans, but also between the diverse social media systems. Again, many other examples exist.

Apart from a growing functionality and interconnectivity of systems, we also want a growing quality of information systems, as industry and society *depend* more and more on their automated systems: where automated systems were an efficiency-increasing 'add-on' in the past, they now form the backbone of operations in many respects. When they stop working, or stop working correctly, many processes come to a grinding halt.

This quickly growing complexity and required quality of systems leads to an also quickly growing need for *structure* of these systems. This is where architecture comes into play: information system architecture provides tools to design and maintain complex, interconnected and dependable information systems on the basis of reliable underlying technology. The complexity of this underlying technology is the focus of software engineering and hardware engineering (remember the various levels of architecture that we have discussed in Section 2.5.2). The fact that architecture grows in importance implies that the importance of the role of IS architect grows in importance. This is a development that is currently observable in many modern organizations, both of the for-profit type and the non-profit type.

Given the growing complexity, architects will be relying more and more on modular thinking: composing solutions for a specific context out of pre-existing partial solutions that are tailored (parameterized, for example) in the right way. This implies at a high level of abstraction that architecture structures will become more important – these are the styles, patterns and reference architectures to which we have given an introduction in Chapter 4 of this book. At a more concrete level, it means that modular information systems will become more important – thereby also increasing the need for good middleware solutions (as discussed in Chapter 9 of this book). To allow all these instruments to develop in the right way, a development of the concepts and theories of IS architecture is a prerequisite. Where architecture in the building construction world has a tradition of several millennia, IS architecture is still in its infancy after only a few decades of proper attention. Much work still remains to be done.

10.2 Challenges of the IS Architect

In Section 2.6, we have introduced the IS architect as an important profession in modern-day organizations and as an important role in the development of business information systems. The IS architect is confronted with a number of challenges that make his/her life hard but interesting. In this section, we briefly discuss the main challenges.

The dichotomy between the business and technology aspects

As discussed in Section 2.7, information system architecture links the business and the IT fields. There are, however, not many professionals in the information systems field who oversee both fields: there is a *practical dichotomy* in the IS field between the business side and the technology side. Hence, the architect often has to bridge the two worlds. This is not always easy, as the architect may be confronted with a project principal who is from one of both fields (or even worse: several consecutive principals who each are from different fields).

The legacy issue

An important challenge for an architect is the fact that many old information systems exist and that they are hard to get rid of – these are the so-called *legacy systems*. These legacy systems can be hard to abandon for several reasons. One reason is the lack of documentation, through which undocumented business knowledge is hidden in software code. A second reason is the lack of modularization of most legacy systems, which makes it hard, or even impossible, to replace them gradually. Another reason is the difference in the life cycles of application systems and infrastructure systems combined with the *n:m* couplings between these two categories of systems.

The dialectics of progress

In designing IS architectures, it is hard to decide when to adopt new standards (for example reference architectures). Being early in the adoption of standards means that the standards may not be fully operational in the field yet and their use hence does not pay off. It may also mean that standards are still susceptible to change. This problem is referred to as the *dialectics of progress*: being ahead of general developments may present itself as a problem. When one is late in the adoption of standards, however, this means that one may miss competitive advantages that are brought by the use of these standards – one may become a laggard.

The invisibility of architecture

Users don't see the structure and hence the complexity of software systems, as these are hidden behind user interfaces. Consequently, IS architectures are invisible to end users and managers of end users [Gre03], who may be important stakeholders in the development of information systems and hence of architectures. The *invisibility* of information system architectures is essentially different from architecture in the building domain, where buildings are easily observable (and even very tangible) in their entirety.

The technology push issue

Information technology has been one of the technological domains with very fast developments – if not the fastest of all (think of the comparison that we have made in Section 2.5.1). And still, new developments in IT come by like pounding waves – take for example the developments of mobile technology in cell phones and tablet computers (and the happy marriage of the two) during the last two decades, or the even more recent developments in the field of artificial intelligence (AI). This means that possibilities of information systems from a technology perspective (technology push) increase quickly: 'what was sci-fi yesterday is possible today and will be old-fashioned tomorrow'. This means that an IS architect must be prepared to deal with *fast and continuous change*.

The growing complexity

And finally, the complexity of (corporate) information systems is an ever growing issue – as already discussed in the first section of this chapter. Fueled by developments like end-to-end business process automation, ubiquitous computing, fully automated e-business, deep integration of social media, autonomous intelligent systems, and many other, the growth of complexity will not soon come to a stop – it may even be subject to an increase of speed. An IS architect must be able to oversee this *growing complexity*.

Figure 133: overseeing complexity (source unknown)

With respect to complexity, the architect working in the building domain has an advantage over the information system architect: in the building domain, the complexity of artifacts (i.e., buildings) is limited by physical constraints – in the information domain, there are no physical constraints. Therefore, information system complexity has been growing and will keep growing.

So is the above all bad news? No, it means that the job of an information system architect is not an easy one – but therefore, it is an interesting one! It combines many aspects, requires multiple skills, and is constantly renewing itself.

11 REFERENCES

[Aal03]   W.M.P van der Aalst, A.H.M. ter Hofstede, B. Kiepuszewski, A.P. Barros; *Workflow Patterns*; Distributed and Parallel Databases, Vol. 14, Nr. 3, 2003; pp. 5-51.

[Abr10]   P. Abrahamsson, M. Ali Babar, P. Kruchten; *Agility and Architecture: Can They Coexist?*; IEEE Software, Vol. 27, No. 2; IEEE, 2010; pp. 16-22.

[Alo04]   G. Alonso, F. Casati, H. Kuno, V. Machiraju; *Web Services: Concepts, Architectures and Applications*; Springer, 2004.

[Ang08]   S. Angelov, P. Grefen; *An E-contracting Reference Architecture*; Journal of Systems and Software; Vol. 81, No. 11; Elsevier, 2008; pp. 1816-1844.

[Ang12]   S. Angelov, P. Grefen, D. Greefhorst; *A Framework for Analysis and Design of Software Reference Architectures*; Information and Software Technology, Vol. 54, No. 4; Elsevier, 2012; pp. 417-431.

[APQ24]   *APQC Process Classification Framework (PCF) - Cross-Industry - Excel Version 7.4*; American Productivity & Quality Center (APQC), 2024.

[Apt02]   N. Apte, T. Mehta; *UDDI: Building Registry-based Web Services Solutions*; Prentice Hall PTR, 2002.

[Bas03]   L. Bass, P. Clements, R. Kazman; *Software Architecture in Practice*; Addison-Wesley, 2003.

[Ber06]   A. Berre, B. Elvesæter, J. Øyvind Aagedal, J. Oldevik, A. Solberg, B. Nordmoen; *COMET: Component and Model-based development Methodology*; SINTEF ICT, 2006.

[Bol01]   F. Bolton; *Pure CORBA*; Sams Publishing, 2001.

[Bor19]   J. Borky, T. Bradley; *Effective Model-Based Systems Engineering*; Springer, 2019.

[Bus96]   F. Buschmann, R. Meunier, H. Rohnert, P. Sommerlad, M. Stal; *Pattern-Oriented Software Architecture Volume 1: A System of Patterns*; Wiley, 1996.

[CEF16] *Reference Data Model (RDM) Guideline*; Buy/Pay Programme Development Area Supply Chain Management, United Nations Centre for Trade Facilitation and Electronic Business, 2016.

[CEF17] *White Paper on a Reference Data Model*; Document ECE/TRADE/C/CEFACT/2017/11; Economic Commission for Europe, Centre for Trade Facilitation and Electronic Business, 2017.

[Cha04] D. Chappell; *Enterprise Service Bus: Theory in Practice*; O'Reilly Media, 2004.

[Cha10] D. Chappell, A. Willis; *The Architect in Practice (10ᵗʰ Edition)*; Wiley-Blackwell, 2010.

[Chi96] F. Ching; *Architecture: Form, Space and Order (2ⁿᵈ Edition)*; Wiley, 1996.

[Clo09] R. Cloutier et al.; *The Concept of Reference Architectures*; Systems Engineering, Vol. 13, No. 1; Wiley, 2009; pp. 14-27.

[Del13] L. Delligatti; *SysML Distilled: A Brief Guide to the Systems Modeling Language*; Addison-Wesley Professional, 2013.

[Die08] J. Dietz; *Architecture – Building Strategy into Design*; Academic Service, 2008.

[Dij16] R. Dijkman, I. Vanderfeesten, H. Reijers; *Business Process Architectures: Overview, Comparison and Framework*; Enterprise Information Systems, Vol. 10, No. 2, 2016; pp. 129-158.

[Elm10] R. Elmasri, S. Navathe; *Fundamentals of Database Systems (6ᵗʰ Edition)*; Addison Wesley, 2010.

[Faj08] J. Fajardo (ed.); *Skin: Architecture & Volume*; Loft Publications, 2008.

[Fet06] P. Fettke, P. Loos, J. Zwicker; *Business Process Reference Models: Survey and Classification*; Proceedings BPM 2005 Workshops; LNCS 3812; Springer, 2006; pp. 469-483.

[Fow10] M. Fowler; *Domain-Specific Languages*; Addison-Wesley, 2010.

[Fow96] M. Fowler; *Analysis Patterns: Reusable Object Models*; Addison-Wesley Professional, 1996.

[Fre19] J. Freund, B. Rücker; *Real-Life BPMN, 4ᵗʰ Edition*; Camunda, 2019.

[Gan79] C. Gane, T. Sarson; *Structured Systems Analysis: Tools and Techniques*; Prentice-Hall, 1979.

[Gre98] P. Grefen, R. Remmerts de Vries; *A Reference Architecture for Workflow Management Systems*; Data & Knowledge Engineering, Vol. 27, No. 1; Elsevier, 1998; pp. 31-57.

[Gre03] P. Grefen; *Onzichtbare Architecturen – tussen Chaos en Structuur in e-Business*; Eindhoven University of Technology, 2003 (text inaugural lecture, in Dutch).

[Gre06] D. Greefhorst, H. Koning, H. van Vliet; *The Many Faces of Architectural Descriptions;* Informations Systems Frontiers, Vol. 2006, No. 8, 2006; pp. 103-113.

[Gre11] D. Greefhorst, E. Proper; *Architecture Principles: The Cornerstones of Enterprise Architecture*; Springer, 2011.

[Gre13] P. Grefen, E. Luftenegger, E. v.d. Linden, C. Weisleder; *BASE/X: Business Agility through Cross-Organizational Service Engineering - The Business and Service Design Approach developed in the CoProFind Project*; Beta Working Papers, Vol. 414; Eindhoven University of Technology, 2013.

[Gre15] P. Grefen; P. Grefen; *Service-Dominant Business Engineering with BASE/X - Practitioner Business Modeling Handbook*; Amazon CreateSpace, 2015; ISBN 978-1516942176.

[Gre16] P. Grefen; *Beyond e-Business*; Routledge; 2016.

[Gre21] P. Grefen, G. Boultadakis; *Designing an Integrated System for Smart Industry: The Development of the HORSE Architecture.* The HORSE Consortium, 2021. ISBN 9-798667-048640.

[GTI14] *Industrie 4.0: Smart Manufacturing for the Future*; Germany Trade & Invest, 2014.

[Han09] D. Hanlon; *Compositions in Architecture*; Wiley, 2009.

[Har07] N. Harrison, P. Avgeriou; *Leveraging Architecture Patterns to Satisfy Quality Attributes*; Proceedings 1st European Conference on Software Architectures; LNCS 4758; Springer, 2007; pp. 263-270.

[Hil07] R. Hilliard; *All About IEEE Std 1471*; ISO Architecture, 2007; available at http://www.iso-architecture.org/ieee-1471/docs/all-about-ieee-1471.pdf (accessed 2024).

[HA16] HORSE Architecture Team; *HORSE Project Deliverable 2.2: Complete System Design*; HORSE Consortium, 2016 (limited dissemination).

[Hol95] D. Hollingsworth; *The Workflow Reference Model*; Workflow Management Coalition, 1995.

[IDS19] *Reference Architecture Model Version 3.0*; International Data Spaces Association, Berlin, Germany, 2019.

[Ite15] *Connected Vehicle Reference Implementation Architecture*; Iteris, 2015; available at http://www.iteris.com/cvria (accessed 2024).

[Jon04] H. Jonkers (ed.) et al.; *Concepts for Architectural Description*; Telematica Instituut, 2004.

[Kae14] H. Kaeslin; *Top-Down Digital VLSI Design: From Architectures to Gate-Level Circuits and FPGAs*; Morgan Kaufmann, 2014.

[Kan03] K. Kandt; *Software Design Principles and Practices*; 2003.

[Kar24] D. Karastoyanova, P. Grefen; *Non-Standard BPM Platforms*; in: P. Grefen, I. Vanderfeesten (eds.); *Handbook on Business Process Management and Digital Transformation*; Edward Elgar, 2024.

[Kau18] O. Kautz, A. Roth, B. Rumpe; *Achievements, Failures, and the Future of Model-Based Software Engineering*; in V. Gruhn, R. Striemer (eds.), *The Essence of Software Engineering*; Springer Open, 2018.

[Kel97] S. Kelly; *Data Warehousing in Action*; Wiley, 1997.

[Kni14] D. Knifton; *Enterprise Data Architecture: How to Navigate its Landscape*; Paragon, 2014.

[Kru95] P. Kruchten; *Architectural Blueprints—The "4+1" View Model of Software Architecture*; IEEE Software, Vol. 12, No. 6; IEEE, 1995; pp. 42-50.

[Lan05] M. Lankorst et al.; *Enterprise Architecture at Work: Modelling, Communication and Analysis*; Springer, 2005.

[Led22] J. Ledin; *Modern Computer Architecture and Organization*; Packt Publishing, 2022.

[Leh80] M. Lehman; *Programs, Life Cycles, and Laws of Software Evolution*; Proceedings of the IEEE, Vol. 68, No. 9; IEEE, 1980; pp. 1060-1076.

[Ley99] F. Leymann, D. Roller; *Production Workflow: Concepts and Techniques*; Prentice Hall, 1999.

[Lin17] Lin, S.; *Industrial Internet Reference Architecture*; Presentation; Industrial Internet Consortium, 2017. Available at https://www.iiconsortium.org/pdf/SHI-WAN%20LIN_IIRA-v1%208-release-20170125.pdf (accessed 2024).

[Lüf12] E. Lüftenegger, P. Grefen, C. Weisleder; *The Service Dominant Strategy Canvas: Towards Networked Business Models*; Proceedings 13th IFIP Working Conference on Virtual Enterprises; Springer, 2012; pp. 207-215.

[Mad10] J. Madison; *Agile–Architecture Interactions*; IEEE Software, Vol. 27, No. 2; IEEE, 2010; pp. 41-48.

[Mai01] M. W. Maier, D. Emery, R. Hilliard; *Software Architecture: Introducing IEEE Standard 1471*; Computer, Vol. 34, No. 4, 2001.

[Mal14] M. Malinova, R. Dijkman, J. Mendling; *Automatic Extraction of Process Categories from Process Model Collections*; Proceedings BPM 2013 Workshops; LNBIP 171; Springer, 2014; pp. 430-441.

[Mar18] R. Martin; *Clean Architecture: A Craftsman's Guide to Software Structure and Design*; Prentice Hall 2018.

[Med00] N. Medvidovic, R. Taylor; *A Classification and Comparison Framework for Software Architecture Description Languages*; IEEE Transactions on Software Engineering, January 2000; pp. 70-93.

[Mil01] J. Miller, J. Mukerji (eds.); *Model Driven Architecture (MDA)*; OMG, 2001.

[Mil06]   R. Miles, K. Hamilton; *Learning UML 2.0*; O'Reilly Media, 2006,

[Min83]   H. Mintzberg; *Structures in Fives: Designing Effective Organizations*; Prentice-Hall, 1983

[Nag21]   M. Nager; *The Smart Student's Guide to Smart Manufacturing and Industry 4.0*; Industrial Insights LLC, 2021.

[New02]   E. Newcomer; *Understanding Web Services: XML, WSDL, SOAP, and UDDI*; Addison-Wesley Professional, 2002.

[New21]   S. Newman; *Building Microservices: Designing Fine-Grained Systems (2nd Edition)*; O'Reilly Media, 2021.

[OM04]   *Common Object Request Broker Architecture: Core Specification, Version 3.0.3*; OMG, 2004.

[OM08]   *MDA Web Site*; OMG, 2008; http://www.omg.org/mda/ (accessed 2024).

[OM15]   *Business Motivation Model Version 1.3*; OMG, 2015.

[Pal08]   A.L. Palmer; *Historical Dictionary of Architecture*; The Scarecrow Press, 2008.

[Pil05]   D. Pilone, N. Pitman; *UML 2.0 in a Nutshell*; O'Reilly Media, 2005.

[Por85]   M. Porter; *Competitive Advantage: Creating and Sustaining Superior Performance*; Free Press, 1985.

[Pou19]   S. Pourmirza, S. Peters, R. Dijkman, P. Grefen; *BPMS-RA: A Novel Reference Architecture for Business Process Management Systems*; ACM Transactions on Internet Technology, Vol. 19, No. 1, Article 13, 2019.

[PW15]   *An Introduction to the European Interoperability Reference Architecture v0.9.0 (EIRA)*; PwC EU Services, 2015.

[Rah17]   P. Raj, A. Raman, H. Subramanian; *Architectural Patterns*; Packt, 2017.

[Sam15]   M. van Sambeek et al.; *Towards an Architecture for Cooperative ITS Applications in the Netherlands*; DITCM, ConnectingMobility, 2015; also available as: Beta Working Papers, Vol. 485; Eindhoven University of Technology; 2015.

[Sch00]   D. Schmidt, M. Stal, H. Rohnert, F. Buschmann; *Pattern-Oriented Software Architecture Volume 2: Patterns for Concurrent and Networked Objects*; Wiley, 2000.

[Sch06]   D. Schmidt; *Model-Driven Engineering*; IEEE Computer, February 2006; IEEE, 2006; pp. 25-31.

[Scr11]   *The Scrum Guide*; Scrum.org, 2011.

[Sha96]   M. Shaw, D. Garlan; *Software Architecture: Perspectives on an Emerging Discipline*; Prentice Hall, 1996.

[Sin21]   T. Sinha; *OLAP vs. OLTP: What's the difference?*; IBM, 2021; available at https://www.ibm.com/think/topics/olap-vs-oltp (accessed 2024).

[Tay10] R. Taylor, N. Medvidovic, E. Dashofy; *Software Architecture: Foundations, Theory, and Practice*; Wiley, 2010.

[Tha99] T. Thai; *Learning DCOM*; O'Reilly Media, 1999.

[Tha00] B. Thalheim; *Entity-Relationship Modeling: Foundations of Database Technology*; Springer, 2000.

[Tho02] E. Thomsen; *OLAP Solutions: Building Multidimensional Information Systems*; Wiley, 2002.

[TOG07] *TOGAF™ The Open Group Architecture Framework – A Management Guide*; Van Haren Publishing, 2007.

[TOG09] *SOA Reference Architecture - Draft Technical Standard*; The Open Group, 2009.

[TOG15] *TOGAF Web Site*; The Open Group; http://www.opengroup.org/togaf/ (accessed 2024).

[TOG16] *ArchiMate 3.0 Reference Cards*; The Open Group, 2016.

[TOG24] The Open Group; *Archimate Web Site*; https://www.opengroup.org/archimate-forum/archimate-overview (inspected 2024).

[Tra21] K. Traganos et al.; *The HORSE framework: A Reference Architecture for Cyber-Physical Systems in Hybrid Smart Manufacturing*; Journal of Manufacturing Systems, Vol. 61; pp. 461-494.

[Tru90] J. Truijens, A. Oosterhaven, R. Maes, H. Jägers, F. van Iersel; *Informatie-infrastructuur: een Instrument voor het Management*; Kluwer Bedrijfswetenschappen, 1990 (in Dutch).

[Tsi78] D. Tsichritzis, A. Klug; *The ANSI/X3/SPARC DBMS Framework Report of the Study Group on Database Management Systems*; Information Systems, Vol. 3, 1978; pp. 173-191.

[Unw10] S. Unwin; *Twenty Buildings Every Architect Should Understand*; Routledge 2010.

[Wie03] R. Wieringa, H. Blanken, M. Fokkinga, P. Grefen; *Aligning Application Architecture to the Business Context*; Proceedings 15th International Conference on Advanced Information Systems Engineering; Springer, 2003; pp. 209-225.

[Wie08] R. Wieringa, P. van Eck, C. Steghuis, E. Proper; *Competences of IT Architects*; Academic Service, 2008.

[Wie21] G. Wierda; *Mastering ArchiMate, Edition 3.1*; R&A, 2021.

[Wi24a] *Zachman Framework*; Wikipedia Article; available at http://en.wikipedia.org/wiki/Zachman_framework (accessed 2024).

[Wi24b] *Vitruvius*; Wikipedia Article; available at http://en.wikipedia.org/wiki/Vitruvius (accessed 2024).

[Wi24c] *Unified Modeling Language*; Wikipedia Article; available at http://en.wikipedia.org/wiki/Unified_Modeling_Language (accessed 2024).

[Wi24d] *The Open Group Architecture Framework*; Wikipedia Article; available at http://en.wikipedia.org/wiki/The_Open_Group_ Architecture_Framework (accessed 2024).

[Wi24e] *NoSQL*; Wikipedia Article; available at http://en.wikipedia.org/wiki/NoSQL (accessed 2024).

[Wi24f] *Lehman's Laws of Software Evolution*; Wikipedia Article; available at https://en.wikipedia.org/wiki/Lehman%27s_laws_of_software_ evolution (accessed 2024).

[Wi24g] *Organizational Chart*; Wikipedia Article; available at https://en.wikipedia.org/wiki/Organizational_chart (accessed 2024).

[Wi24h] *Solution Stack*; Wikipedia Article; available at https://en.wikipedia.org/wiki/Solution_stack (accessed 2024).

[Wi24i] *Data-Flow Diagram*; Wikipedia Article; available at https://en.wikipedia.org/wiki/Data-flow_diagram (accessed 2024).

[Wi24j] *ArchiMate*; Wikipedia Article; available at https://en.wikipedia.org/wiki/ArchiMate (accessed 2024).

[Wi24k] *COBOL*; Wikipedia Article; available at https://en.wikipedia.org/wiki/COBOL (accessed 2024).

[Wi24l] *Distributed Component Object Model*; Wikipedia Article; available at https://en.wikipedia.org/wiki/Distributed_Component_Object_Model (accessed 2024).

[Wi24m] *OSI Model*; Wikipedia Article; available at https://en.wikipedia.org/wiki/OSI_model (accessed 2024).

[Wi24n] *CODASYL*; Wikipedia Article; available at https://en.wikipedia.org/wiki/CODASYL (accessed 2024).

[Woo15] A. Wood; *100 of the World's Tallest Buildings*; Council on Tall Buildings and Urban Habitat, Images Publishing, 2015.

[Zac02] J. Zachman; *The Zachman Framework for Enterprise Architecture*; Zachman International, 2002.

[Zhu05] H. Zhu; *Software Design Methodology: From Principles to Architectural Styles*; Butterworth-Heinemann, 2005.

[Zim23] O. Zimmerman et al.; *Patterns for API Design: Simplifying Integration with Loosely Coupled Message Exchanges*; Addison-Wesly, 2023.

12 ABOUT THE AUTHOR

Paul Grefen is a senior full professor in the School of Industrial Engineering at Eindhoven University of Technology (TU/e) in the Netherlands. He received his Ph.D. in Computer Science from the University of Twente, also in the Netherlands. He was a visiting researcher at Stanford University in the USA, IBM Almaden Research Center in the USA, Smeal College of Business of Penn State University in the USA, and KU Leuven in Belgium.

He has been involved in leading roles in many European and national research projects, mostly in collaboration with industry. He is an editor and author of the books on the European WIDE, CrossWork, and HORSE projects, and has authored books on business process management, electronic business, service-dominant business engineering, information systems, and blockchain.

His current research covers digital transformation, architectural design of business systems, inter-organizational business process management and service-oriented business engineering.

He is part-time employed at Eviden Digital Transformation Consulting as a principal architect in the smart industry domain. He teaches at TIAS business school. He is the research director of the European Supply Chain Forum. His company G.DBA advises organizations on digital transformation and digital business architecture.

13 INDEX

3

3-tier · 134

4

4-tier · 133

A

abstraction
  dimension · 53
  functional · 74
ADM · *See* TOGAF Architecture
  Development Method
aggregation
  dimension · 44
agile
  architecture · 126
  development · 125
ANSI/SPARC · 102
API · *See* application programming
  interface
  -based architecture · 81
application architect · 143
application programming interface
  · 81
APQC · 111
ArchiMate · 121

  domain · 121
architect · 22
  application · 22, 143
  challenges · 196
  infrastructure · 22, 143
architecture
  stratified · 39
aspect
  dimension · 28

B

batch sequential · 92
black board · 92
BMPN · 37
BOAT
  framework · 59
BPEL · 188
BPMN · 34, 170
BPMS · 140, 169, *See* business
  process management system
BPMS-RA · 105
brownfield
  situation · 8
business intelligence · 169
Business Motivation Model · 60
Business Process Execution
  Language · *See* BPEL
business process framework · 111
business process management
  system · 35
business rule · 95

C

call & return · 92
case management system · 170
catalog
    architecture design principles · 128
    software architecture patterns · 89
CEFACT · 110
client stub · 184
client/server system · 167
club administration · 32
CODASYL · 168
COMET · 127
Common Object Request Broker
    Architecture · See CORBA
communicating processes · 92
component diagram · 33
contractor · 23
CORBA · 106, 182
COTS · 165

D

data architecture · 32
data centered · 92
data dimension class · 97
data fabric · 169
data flow · 92
data flow diagram · 34
data model
    object-oriented · 169
    relational · 169
    star · 97
DBMS · 140, 166
DCOM · 186
decision support system · 147
demand pull · 10
dialectics of progress · 197
distributed object architecture ·
    164, 182
DOA · See distributed object
    architecture
domain-specific language · 165

DSS · See decision support system

E

e-business information system · 45
EIRA · 108
EIS · 45
enterprise architect · 143
enterprise information system · 45
enterprise resource planning · 35
enterprise resource planning
    system · 45, 165
enterprise service bus · 190
ERA · 102
ERP · 45, See enterprise resource
    planning
ERP system · 6
ESB · 140, 190
ETL · See extraction and
    transformation logic
European Interoperability
    Reference Architecture · 108
event system · 92
extended enterprise information
    system · 45
eXtended Markup Language · See
    XML
extraction and transformation
    logic · 148

F

facts class · 97
financial information system · 33
framework · 116
    Kruchten · 40
    Truijens · 29
    Zachman · 117

G

Gehry, Frank · 2

greenfield
    problem · 9
    situation · 8, 9

H

Hadid, Zaha · 18
HTTP · 188
HyperText Transfer Protocol · *See*
    HTTP

I

IDL · 185
IIOP · 184
IIRA · *See* Industrial Internet
    Reference Architecture
independent components · 92
Industrial Internet Reference
    Architecture · 102
infrastructure · 131
infrastructure architect · 143
Interface Definition Language · *See*
    IDL
Internet Inter-ORB Protocol · *See*
    IIOP
Internet of Things · 24
interpreter · 93
IoT · *See* Internet of Things
ISO-OSI model · 75

K

K4+1 · *See* Kruchten Framework
Kruchten framework · 40

L

legacy · 6
    problem · 8, 9
    situation · 123, 191

    system · 197
    type · 168
legacy problem · 168
Lehman's laws · 10

M

machine bureaucracy · 9
manufacturing · 34
manufacturing execution system ·
    35
manufacturing process control
    system · 35
manufacturing process
    management system · 35
MBSE · *See* model-based systems
    engineering
MDA · 119
MDE · *See* model-driven
    engineering
Mercurius · 103, 152
MES · *See* manufacturing execution
    system
message broker · 182
microarchitecture · 20
microservice architecture · 81
middleware · 177
    database-oriented · 179
    function-oriented · 180
    message-oriented · 181
    object-oriented · 182
    service-oriented · 187
Mintzberg · 9
MMDBMS · 169
mobility service · 109
model-based systems engineering ·
    119
model-driven engineering · 119
modularity · 139
    horizontal · 78
    vertical · 76
MPMS · *See* manufacturing process
    management system

N

NoSQL · 169
not-invented-here syndrome · 165

O

object client · 183
object management architecture · 182
Object Management Group · 105, 119, 121
object request broker · 106, 183
object server · 183
offshoring · 24
OLAP · 140, 169, *See* online analytical processing
OLTP · 140
OMA · 105, 185, *See* object management architecture
OMG · 105, 119, 121, 185
online analytical processing · 147
OODBMS · 169
Open Group · 122
ORB · 186, *See* object request broker
ORBIX · 186
organogram · 34, 39

P

pattern · 88
    catalogue · 91
PCF · *See* process classification framework
pipes & filters · 92
PLMS · *See* product lifecycle management system
Porter · 136, 159
process architecture · 32
process classification framework · 111

product lifecycle management system · 35
professional bureaucracy · 9
program & subroutine · 93

Q

quality attribute · 87

R

RDBMS · 169
RDM · *See* Reference Data Model
realization
    dimension · 59
reference architecture · 100
Reference Architecture
    SOA · 106
reference data models · 110
reference model · 100
registry · 188
remote procedure call · 180
repository · 92
requirements pull · 10, 24, 142
RFID · 24
RPC · *See* remote procedure call
rule-based system · 93

S

Scrum · 125
serializable · 167
server skeleton · 184
service-oriented architecture · 81, 190
silo · 6
Simple Object Access Protocol · *See* SOAP
single point of truth · 146
smart manufacturing · 34
SOA · *See* service-oriented architecture

SOAP · 188
software stack · 34
solution stack · 34
sprint · 125
SQL · 169
standard architecture · 112
standardization · 128
stratum · 75
style · 73
    columned · 77
    component-oriented · 80
    layered · 74
    monolithic · 73
    object-oriented · 81
    service-oriented · 81
    stratified · 75
SysML · 34

T

technical architect · 143
technology push · 10, 24, 142
technology stack · 34
The Open Group · 106
three-tier · 133
tier · 133
TOGAF · 126
    Architecture Development Method
        · 126
transaction · 167
Truijens framework · 29
    updated · 31

U

UDDI · 188
UML · 32
Uniform Resource Locator · *See*
    URL
Universal Description, Discovery
    and Integration · *See* UDDI
URL · 188

UT5 · *See* updated Truijens
    framework

V

value chain model · 136
virtual machine · 93
Vitruvius · 16
VLSI · 20

W

web service · 187
Web Service Definition Language ·
    See WSDL
WfMC · 151, *See* Workflow
    Management Coalition
WFMS · 140
what-if analysis · 148
Workflow Management Coalition ·
    102, 151
wrapping · 192
WS Coordination · *See* WS-C
WS Transaction · *See* WS-T
WS-Agreement · 188
WS-C · 188
WSDL · 188
WS-Security · 188
WS-T · 188

X

XML · 188

Z

Zachman · 117

14 Table of
Figures

Figure 1: Guggenheim Museum, Bilbao, Spain, designed by Frank Gehry (photo by author) 2

Figure 2: structure of this book 4

Figure 3: forces in information system development (adapted from [Gre03]) 10

Figure 4: the two faces of architecture with some of their relations 12

Figure 5: an example of ancient Greek architecture (source unknown) 17

Figure 6: modern architecture applied in building: top station of the Hungerburgbahn in Innsbruck, Austria, designed by Zaha Hadid (photo by author) 18

Figure 7: IBM RAMAC 305 System (photo via Norsk Teknisk Museum) 19

Figure 8: software, CIS and enterprise architecture as a spectrum....................22

Figure 9: the architect overseeing and communicating between groups of stakeholders in an IS development project 23

Figure 10: technology push and requirements pull forces in system evolution..25

Figure 11: architecture (A) as a pivot between business and organization on the one hand, and technology on the other hand (adapted from [Gre16]) 25

Figure 12: 5 aspects framework according to [Tru90] 30

Figure 13: modernized variation on the Truijens framework (UT5)..................31

Figure 14: simple example of a UML class diagram for the data architecture aspect (source unknown) 33

Figure 15: simple example of a UML component diagram for the system architecture aspect 34

Figure 16: software aspect context architecture of example manufacturing CIS 35

Figure 17: high-level data aspect architecture of example MPMS....................36

Figure 18: process aspect architecture of example manufacturing CIS 38

Figure 19: high-level platform aspect architecture of example manufacturing CIS 39

Figure 20: organization aspect architecture of example manufacturing CIS 40

Figure 21: 4+1 aspect framework according to [Kru95]................................... 41

Figure 22: example set of aggregation levels.. 44

Figure 23: example abstract architecture aggregation level 1 46

Figure 24: example abstract architecture aggregation level 2........................... 47

Figure 25: example abstract architecture aggregation level 3........................... 47

Figure 26: TOA OMIS architecture at Aggregation Level 1 48

Figure 27: TOA OMIS architecture at Aggregation Level 2 48

Figure 28: TOA OMIS architecture at Aggregation Level 3 49

Figure 29: MPCS software architecture at aggregation level 1 49

Figure 30: MCS software architecture at aggregation level 2........................... 50

Figure 31: MCS software architecture at aggregation level 3........................... 51

Figure 32: MCS software architecture at aggregation level 4........................... 52

Figure 33: example architecture model at abstraction level 0........................... 55

Figure 34: example architecture model abstraction level 1 55

Figure 35: example architecture model at abstraction level 2........................... 56

Figure 36: example architecture model at abstraction level 4........................... 56

Figure 37: data aspect element at abstraction *level 2* 57

Figure 38: data aspect element at abstraction *level 3* 57

Figure 39: data aspect element at abstraction *level 4* 58

Figure 40: BOAT model [(taken from [Gre16])] 59

Figure 41: all four architecture dimensions combined...................................... 61

Figure 42: architecture specification positioned in four-dimensional design space.. 62

Figure 43: three dimensions combined 63

Figure 44: architecture cube with one cell opened 64

Figure 45: example path through the cube... 65

Figure 46: alternative example path through the cube 66

Figure 47: cube with realization dimension implicit and software aspect highlighted 67

Figure 48: three alternative design paths for the software aspect 68

Figure 49: aspect slice expanded into a cube for the realization dimension 69

Figure 50: Doric, Ionic and Corinthian column styles [(sources unknown)] 72

Figure 51: basic IS architecture styles 74

Figure 52: structure of an architecture with a layered style 75

Figure 53: layering in building architecture: the levels of the Louvre in Paris, realized in different building periods (photo by author) 76

Figure 54: example architecture with layered style 77

Figure 55: columned style 78

Figure 56: columned style in an abstract house floor plan 78

Figure 57: example architecture with columned style 79

Figure 58: columned version of the architecture of Figure 15 80

Figure 59: illustration of the component-oriented style 80

Figure 60: simple example architecture with service-oriented style 82

Figure 61: abstract example of component-oriented style in layered style ... 83

Figure 62: example architecture in a component-oriented style 84

Figure 63: example architecture in a layered style 85

Figure 64: example architecture in a columned style 86

Figure 65: two patterns for connecting rooms in a building: linear (left) and star-shaped (right) 88

Figure 66: very basic pattern catalog in graphical form 90

Figure 67: bigger pattern catalogue for system aspect (based on [Bas03]) 92

Figure 68: pipe & filter pattern in application example 96

Figure 69: repository pattern in application example 97

Figure 70: star data pattern principle (based on [Kell97]) 98

Figure 71: star data pattern example for retail (based on [Kell97]) 98

Figure 72: example of semi-detached houses with slanted roof (source unknown) 99

Figure 73: reference architecture process 101

Figure 74: WfMC reference architecture for WFMS (from [Hol95]) 103

Figure 75: Mercurius reference architecture for WFMS, aggregation level 1 .. 104

Figure 76: Mercurius reference architecture for WFMS, WF Server part of aggregation level 2 104

Figure 77: basic Object Management Architecture 106

Figure 78: The Open Group SOA Reference Architecture overview (taken from [TOG09]) 107

Figure 79: High-level overview of EIRA (taken from [PW15]) 108

Figure 80: Technical view of Dutch C-ITS reference architecture (taken from [Sam15]) 109

Figure 81: example Master Data Exchange Structure (taken from [CEF16]) 111

Figure 82: the relation between reference and standard architectures 112

Figure 83: architecting process elements 116

Figure 84: Zachman Framework for Enterprise Architecture (taken from [Wi24a]) ... 118

Figure 85: MDA framework (taken from [OM08]) 119

Figure 86: simple insurance claim architecture in ArchiMate (extended from [Wi24j]) 122

Figure 87: concurrent aspect architecture design 124

Figure 88: phased aspect architecture design 125

Figure 89: example architecture principle from a catalog of principles (from [Gre11]) 129

Figure 90: applications and infrastructure paraphrased: trains on tracks at Maastricht Central Station (photo by author) 132

Figure 91: application and infrastructure layers in context 133

Figure 92: 3-tier (left) and 4-tier (right) architecture structures 134

Figure 93: 3-tier and 4-tier structures with infrastructure layer 135

Figure 94: adapted version of Porter's value chain model 136

Figure 95: application layer structure conforming to Figure 94 on top of infrastructure layer 138

Figure 96: information system modules in application columns, with HRM column detailed 138

Figure 97: airline information system modules in application columns, with Operations column detailed 139

Figure 98: infrastructure layer structure (bottom two layers) supporting application layer (top layer) 141

Figure 99: architects and layers 143

Figure 100: data warehousing reference architecture 147

Figure 101: DW reference architecture in a columned style 148

Figure 102: high-level TOA concrete data warehousing architecture 149

Figure 103: TOA concrete data warehousing architecture 150

Figure 104: WfMC reference architecture for workflow management systems 151

Figure 105: model at the third aggregation level of the Mercurius reference architecture 153

Figure 106: concrete BPM architecture (insurance firm) 154

Figure 107: example TOA application system landscape architecture 155

Figure 108: example interoperability pattern in TOA application architecture 157

Figure 109: example interoperability patterns in TOA application architecture 158

Figure 110: refined version of the TOA application architecture 159

Figure 111: application system architecture in the context of enterprise system architecture 160

Figure 112: illustration of chaotic enterprise system architecture (to avoid!) . 161

Figure 113: architecture of a database management system 167

Figure 114: architecture of a client/server database management system 168

Figure 115: place of embodiment in the IS development cube 171

Figure 116: connectivity in an application landscape 174

Figure 117: possible interfaces within a simple application layer...................175

Figure 118: application layer organized with middleware 176

Figure 119: possible interfaces between application layer and infrastructure layer 176

Figure 120: application and infrastructure layer connected by middleware.....177

Figure 121: database-oriented middleware in a system landscape..................180

Figure 122: illustration of the RPC mechanism 181

Figure 123: OMA/CORBA basic architecture. 183

Figure 124: basic CORBA inter-object mechanism..184

Figure 125: technical communication in OMA/CORBA 185

Figure 126: dual focus of IDL...185

Figure 127: terminology around CORBA 186

Figure 128: a Web Service technology stack 187

Figure 129: simple application scenario with Web Service standards 189

Figure 130: ESB in CIS...190

Figure 131: integrating the old and the new: the Royal Library in Copenhagen with the old wing to the far left and the new wing (called the Black Diamond) to the right (photo by author) 192

Figure 132: wrapping of legacy systems in a CORBA context.......................193

Figure 133: overseeing complexity (source unknown) 198

www.ingramcontent.com/pod-product-compliance
Lightning Source LLC
LaVergne TN
LVHW052127070326
832902LV00039B/1881